Peking Opera Master
Zhang Junqiu

京剧大师

张君秋

天津市中华民族文化促进会
天津市张君秋艺术基金会 编辑
天津杨柳青画社 出版

《京剧大师张君秋》编辑委员会

总策划	李瑞环
策　划	方　放　谢虹雯
主　编	叶厚荣
副主编	安志强　高长德
编　委	（以姓氏笔划为序）
	叶厚荣　安志强　刘雪涛　刘同达　何顺信　李宗鑫
	张学津　张学浩　经　平　高长德　蔡英莲　薛亚萍
文字编撰	安志强
责任编辑	刘建超　杨　文
英文翻译	廖　涛
责任校对	刘　见　刘宏伟
技术编辑	赵润平　张　明　江　楠
装帧设计	陈幼林工作室
资料提供	中国戏曲学院、北京京剧院、中国艺术研究院、天津市中华民族文化促进会、天津市张君秋艺术基金会、天津市青年京剧团、天津图书馆、南开大学图书馆、天津市周恩来邓颖超纪念馆《中国京剧》杂志社和赵景勃、王玉珍、王文章、刘雪涛、何顺信、黄宗江、陆行素、陆继英、蔡英莲、陈娟美、单耀珠、刘长江、戴天平、张庭萱、白晶环、曹　侃、张学治、葛子平、林瑞康等

Editorial Committee of "Peking Opera Master-- Zhang Jun-qiu"

General Planning Editor: Li Rui-huan
Planning Editors: Fang Fang, Xie Hong-wen
Editor-in-chief: Ye Hou-rong
Vice Editors-in-chief: An Zhi-qiang, Gao Chang-de
Committee Members: Ye Hou-rong, An Zhi-qiang, Liu Xue-tao, Liu Tong-da, He Shun-xin, Li Zong-xin, Zhang Xue-jin, Zhang Xue-hao, Jing Ping, Gao Chang-de, Cai Ying-lian, Xue Ya-ping
Compiler: An Zhi-qiang
Executive Editors: Liu Jian-chao, Yang Wen
Translator: Liao Tao
Executive Revisers: Liu Jian, Liu Hong-wei
Technical Editor: Zhao Run-ping, Zhang Ming, Jiang Nan
Designer: Chen you-lin Design studio
Sources: Academy of Chinese Traditional Opera, Beijing Peking Opera Theatre, Academy of Chinese Art, Tianjin Chinese National Culture Promotion Association, Tianjin Zhang Jun-qiu Art Fund, Tianjin Young Peking Opera Troupe, Tianjin Library, Library of Nankai University, Tianjin Zhou En-lai and Deng Ying-chao Memorial, Chinese Peking Opera Press, Zhao Jing-bo, Wang Yu-zhen, Wang Wen-zhang, Liu Xue-tao, He Shun-xin, Huang Zong-jiang, Lu Xing-su, Lu Ji-ying, Cai Ying-lian, Chen Juan-mei, Shan Yao-zhu, Liu Chang-jiang, Dai Tian-ping, Zhang Ting-xuan, Bai Jing-huan, Cao Kan, Zhang Xue-zhi, Ge Zi-ping and Lin Rui-kang.

目录

- 007　李瑞环同志题词
- 009　张君秋像
- 011　序　　李瑞环
- 015　张君秋生平
- 019　中央领导同张君秋
- 025　张君秋艺术形象

求学篇
- 051　苦难童年
- 054　拜师学艺
- 057　崭露头角

求索篇
- 071　博采众长
- 087　自组班社
- 096　香港之旅

创新篇
- 105　重焕青春
- 112　推陈出新
- 125　唱腔创新
- 129　创立张派

育人篇
- 183　菊园耕耘
- 201　襄助"集训"
- 208　门墙桃李

配像篇
- 227　任重道远
- 230　呕心沥血
- 248　"配像"丰碑

交游篇
- 257　艺播四海
- 274　博识多才
- 290　良师益友
- 306　闲情逸趣

流芳篇
- 319　身后哀荣
- 324　音容宛在

- 331　张君秋生平大事年表
- 348　后记

CONTENTS

- 007   Epigraph by Comrade Li Rui-huan
- 009   The picture of Zhang Jun-qiu
- 011   Preface (Li Rui-huan)
- 015   Biography
- 019   Party leader and Zhang Jun-qiu
- 025   Zhang Jun-qiu's Artistic Images

Study

- 051   Miserable Childhood
- 054   Taking a Master to Learn a Craft
- 057   Beginning to Show His Brilliant Talents

Pursuit

- 071   Learning from Others
- 087   The Establishment of His Own Troupe
- 096   Tour in Hong Kong

Innovation

- 105   Another Bloom of Youth
- 112   Weeding Through the Old to Bring Forth the New
- 125   Innovation of Aria
- 129   The Foundation of Zhang School

Education Career

- 183   Cultivation of the Young Generation
- 201   Indirect Help to the 100-day Training
- 208   A Roomful of Students

Achievements of Audio Video Tapes

- 227   Shouldering Heavy Responsibility
- 230   Working His Heart Out
- 248   Imperishable Masterpiece

Keeping Companion with Others

- 257   The Worldwide Spread of His Art
- 274   Being of Great Learning and Great Ability
- 290   Mentors
- 306   Leisurely and Carefree Mood

Immortality

- 319   Posthumous Fame
- 324   Being Remembered Forever

- 331   Lifetime Events of Zhang Jun-qiu
- 348   Postscript

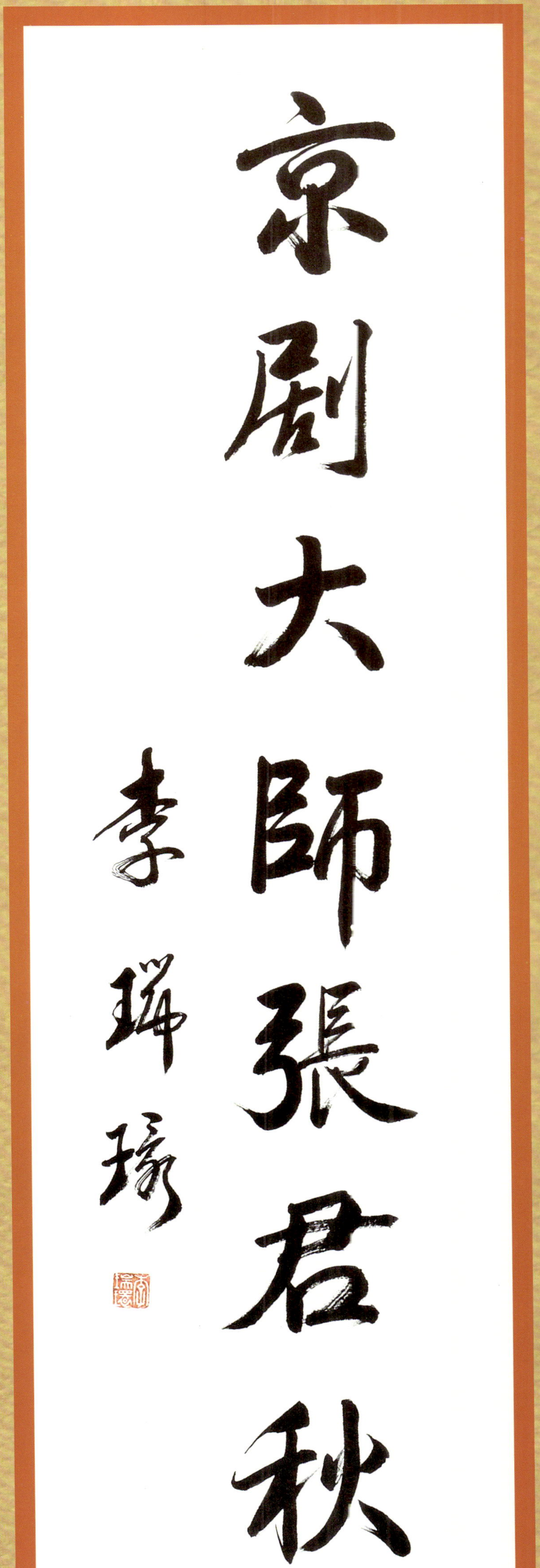

京剧大师张君秋

李瑞环

李瑞环同志题词："京剧大师张君秋"

张君秋（1920~1997）
Zhang Jun-qiu (1920~1997)

序

李瑞环

今年是我国的京剧大师张君秋同志诞辰85周年。君秋同志离开我们也已经8年了。根据京剧界和其他文化界朋友的希望，我要天津市中华民族文化促进会和天津市张君秋艺术基金会为君秋同志编辑出版一本画册、举办几场纪念演出、召开一次研究继承弘扬张派艺术的会议，以纪念君秋同志。

《京剧大师张君秋》画册，汇集了600多张弥足珍贵的照片，这是从广泛征集来的2000多张照片中精心挑选出来的，还有许多难得一见的图片与资料，比较全面地展现了君秋同志光辉绚丽的一生。

君秋同志的一生，是为繁荣京剧艺术事业奋斗不息的一生。我们纪念君秋同志，最重要的是认真继承他的遗愿，学习他的精湛艺术，弘扬他的高尚风范，把他毕生执著追求的京剧事业振兴起来。

要像君秋同志那样勇于在继承的基础上创新，把京剧艺术很好地继承下来，不断发扬光大。君秋同志天赋好，肯用功，又经多位名家指教，年轻时即唱红大江南北，但他从不满足，而是认真借鉴不同流派，博采众长，融会贯通，结合自身条件，创造了风格独特的张派艺术，把京剧旦角艺术推向了一个新的高峰。近几年出版发行的张君秋唱腔集，《中国京剧音配像精粹·张君秋专辑》和张君秋影像资料集，展现出君秋同志在剧坛耕耘一生的辉煌成果，是他为京剧艺术和中华民族文化留下的宝贵财富。我们要大力弘扬张派艺术，更要学习君秋同志艺无止境的精神，刻苦练功学艺，牛在继承前人成果的基础上有所创新，使京剧艺术这一中华民族文化瑰宝放射出更加璀璨的光辉。

要像君秋同志那样乐于奖掖后进，把全部心力投入到培养青年一代，使京剧事业后继有人。君秋同志广收弟子，桃李满天下。粉碎

"四人帮"以后，为了改变"文革"造成的京剧演员、剧目、观众严重断档的局面，他更毅然把主要精力放在京剧教育事业上。他不仅无私地传授张派艺术，而且由于他的丰富经历和机缘，熟悉京剧的各个行当，特别是每个剧目的总体配合和效果，因而他在多方面的京剧教学指导中发挥了重要作用。天津市青年京剧团能演出许多台高水平的大戏，拥有一批全国公认的优秀演员，可以说驰名海内外，这一切得益于君秋同志指导的"百日集训"、得益于他和一大批老艺术家的悉心传授。京剧音配像精粹对京剧的抢救、普及、教学、振兴以及保存、流传具有重大的意义，在中央电视台久播不衰，为广大戏迷观众所喜爱，被普遍认为是前所未有的一大创造，是弘扬民族优秀文化的一大工程，而这项工程就是以君秋同志为总顾问，在他的积极操办下开创的。他亲自指导录制的音配像有120部，涉及诸多京剧艺术流派，现仍在继续录制，并推行到评剧、曲艺等其他剧种。君秋同志垂暮之年，发挥晚霞余辉，为振兴京剧艺术夜以继日、呕心沥血，做出了不可磨灭的贡献。我们要学习他这种鞠躬尽瘁、死而后已的精神，把他的未竟事业继续下去，使京剧人才辈出，使京剧事业代代相传，永葆青春。

要像君秋同志那样处事为人，加强思想修养，做到德艺双馨。君秋同志为人忠厚，助人为乐，谦虚谨慎，豁达大度，团结同志。他对待同志诚恳热情，对待工作一丝不苟。他做人人格好，演戏戏德高，当党员党性强，在京剧界、在艺术家当中有口皆碑。在君秋同志身上，体现了老艺术家的高风亮节和共产党员的优良品德。我们要学习他的崇高风范，在不同的工作岗位上努力做一个脱离低级趣味、有益于人民的人。

2005年6月

Preface

Li Rui-huan

This year is the 85th anniversary of the birth of Peking Opera master Zhang Jun-qiu. Our respected artist passed away 8 years ago. It is of the expectations of the walks of Peking Opera and the friends from other fields that I asked the Tianjin Chinese National Cultural Promotion Association and Tianjin Zhang Jun-qiu Art Fund to publish a picture album, to hold several performances and to convene a seminar on the inheritance and promotion of the school of Zhang Jun-qiu to commemorate him.

The picture album *Peking Opera Master-Zhang Jun-qiu* includes more than 600 meticulously selected photos of Zhang from 2000 widely collected ones, and many other rarely seen pictures and materials, all of which comprehensively display Zhang Jun-qiu's brilliant life.

He has devoted all his life to the prosperity of Peking Opera. In commemoration of Zhang Jun-qiu, we should vitalize the undertakings that he had pursued all his life through the inheritance of his will, the acquirement of his consummate mastery of art and the promotion of his lofty morality.

We should carry on the art of Peking Opera, just like what Zhang Jun-qiu had done, in the manner of creativity based on inheritance. Although quite gifted in art, he was a hardworking student. Instructed by several noted teachers, he became well-known in China when he was quite young. Being a person who was keen on learning, he formed the unique Zhang School by digesting other schools' strong points to combine with its own advantages, thus pushing the role of Dan in Peking Opera to a new stage. Zhang Jun-qiu's aria collections published in recent years, such as *Peking Opera Audio-videotaped Classics • Zhang Jun-qiu Special Album* and the audio video album of Zhang Jun-qiu, both demonstrating Zhang Jun-qiu's glorious lifetime legacy on the stage, are the precious treasure he left for Peking Opera and Chinese culture. We should not only greatly promote the art of "Zhang School", but also his infinite learning spirit to enrich the art of Peking Opera, which is the cultural treasure of Chinese people through creativity on the basis of the existing achievements.

Zhang Jun-qiu also paid a lot of attention to the cultivation of the young generation to ensure that there will be follwers to carry on this career. He had students in every nook

and cranny of the world. During the Cultural Revolution, there was a scarcity of Peking Opera actors' actresses and plays, and people were unwilling to see Peking Opera. To reverse this situation, Zhang Jun-qiu decided to focus his energy on the education of this art. He unselfishly taught many talents the essence of Zhang School. Owing to his abundant experiences in this art, his familiarity with various schools of Peking Opera and its plays, his role in the teaching of Peking Opera was quite indispensable. The reason why Tianjin Young Peking Opera Troupe can present so many first class performances, has so many well-known excellent actors and actresses and becomes so famous both at home and abroad is quite closely connected with the guidance of our respected Zhang and other senior artists. To audio-videotape the classics of Peking Opera is deemed as an effective way in saving, popularizing, vitalizing and keeping this kind of treasure. The broadcasting of the audio-videotapes in CCTV, China Central Television, is quite popular among millions of TV viewers. The audio-videotaping project is universally recognized as an unprecedented invention and also a grand event to pass down Chinese excellent culture' the senior counselor of which is Zhang Jun-qiu. He engaged in audio-videotaping of 120 Peking Opera plays covering various schools. This project is still being carried on even though Zhang passed away, and other operas are also being audio-videotaped, such as Pingju opera. Zhang Jun-qiu exerted utmost efforts to invigorate the undertaking of Peking Opera and has made inerasable contributions. What we need to learn is his attitude in sparing no efforts in the performance of his duty, and in carrying on his unaccomplished mission of nurturing more talented Peking Opera performers in order to make this undertaking prosperous.

To learn the way he treated people and to improve our moral level will enable us to be morally and professionally respectable. Zhang Jun-qiu is noted for his integrity, honesty, modesty, prudence, tolerance and solidarity and he is always ready to help others. He always treated his colleague in a sincere and pure-hearted manner, and handled his work with great meticulosity. His lofty personality, great professional morality and his leading role as a CPC (Communist Party of China) member won him universal praise in the walks of Peking Opera. He embodied the good qualities of a senior artist and virtues of a CPC member. Our learning of his lofty manner at work will transform us into the kind of person above vulgar interests and beneficial to people.

June, 2005

张君秋生平

张君秋原名滕家鸿,祖籍江苏丹徒。1920年10月14日(农历庚申年九月初三)生于北京。父滕联芳。母张秀琴,河北梆子青衣演员。在母亲的影响下,自幼热爱戏曲艺术。1933年,拜师李凌枫,开始学习京剧青衣。1936年初首次登台,先后在雷喜福、王又宸、孟小冬、马连良、谭富英等班社搭班演出。不到20岁就以俊美的扮相,天赋的佳喉,深受观众的青睐,红遍大江南北。1942年,自组谦和社,担任主演。从艺期间,得到王瑶卿、尚小云、梅兰芳、程砚秋等名家的指点与亲授,认真继承前辈艺术,深入钻研各种流派艺术,在《凤双栖》《怜香伴》等新编剧目中进行了初步的创新探索。1948年,同马连良、俞振飞至香港演出并拍摄戏曲影片。因战事阻隔,困居香港。1951年10月,在周恩来总理的直接关怀下回到内地,参加中南京剧团。1952年,在北京组建北京市京剧三团。1956年,同马连良、谭富英、裘盛戎等组建北京京剧团(现北京京剧院)。

50年代中期至60年代中期是张君秋艺术的鼎盛时期。张君秋认真继承了梅、尚、程、荀等名家的艺术成就,博采众长,结合自己的特点和优势,创造了风格独特的张派艺术。在剧目上,他本着"去芜存菁"的精神,整理演出了《刘兰芝》(原《孔雀东南飞》)、《起解、会审》、《春秋配》、《银屏公主》、《大保国、探皇灵、二进宫》、《红鬃烈马》、《四郎探母》、《金山寺、断桥、雷峰塔》等大量传统戏,并对自己曾经创作演出的《怜香伴》做进一步的加工整理,使这些戏在艺术上有了新的面貌;创作演出了一批历史戏和京剧现代戏,如《刘兰芝》、《彩楼记》、《珍妃》、《望江亭》、《西厢记》、《诗文会》、《楚宫恨》、《秦香莲》、《状元媒》、《秋瑾》、《赵氏孤儿》、《年年有余》等,使之成为深受观众喜爱的张派代表剧目。在这些剧目的演出中,他以独特的艺术视角,自然率真的表演,声情并茂的演唱,表现了中国妇女的聪明才智以及对旧社会恶势力的抗争勇气,塑造了众多生动的舞台形象。在唱腔上,他充分运用自己嗓音圆润、音域宽阔的天赋特长,创造了大量的新腔。他十分注重人物内心情感的深入挖掘,以传统唱腔为基础,悉心揣摩不同流派的艺术风韵,吸收其他行当及兄弟剧种、曲艺、歌曲的音乐语汇，加以融会贯通，充分发挥了"娇、媚、脆、水"的演唱特色和魅力，形成了华丽柔美、刚健清新的演唱风格。

在表演上他功底深厚，化妆、服饰讲究色调款式同人物身份、处境的协调，力求创新，使得他所扮演的人物端庄大方，自然含蓄，风姿绰约，仪态万方。所有这些艺术创造，都充满了浓厚的时代气息，增添了京剧艺术的感染力，使得他的演出生动传神，美视美听，受到广大京剧观众的热烈欢迎，得到京剧行家的一致赞许，被称誉为张派艺术并得以广泛流传。张派艺术的形成和传播，对京剧旦角乃至整个京剧艺术都具有深远的影响，是新中国京剧艺术在新时代取得辉煌发展的重要标志。

"文革"十年中，张君秋的身心受到了严重摧残，但他对于中国共产党的信念始终不渝。粉碎"四人帮"后，张君秋恢复了舞台生活，积极参加社会活动，出任中国戏曲学院副院长。1981年6月，加入中国共产党。先后被选为第五届政协委员，第六、七、八届全国政协常务委员，第四、五届全国文联副主席，全国剧协副主席，中国京剧艺术基金会名誉会长。

张君秋在晚年怀着对振兴京剧的高度责任感，发挥了老一辈艺术家不可替代的作用，做出了巨大贡献。面对经过十年浩劫，京剧事业受到严重摧残、京剧人才严重断档的局面，他毅然把主要精力放在培养青年京剧演员的戏曲教育事业上。他不仅在中国戏曲学院的建设上献计出力，著书立说，出色地完成了教学工作，而且广收弟子，为京剧事业培养更多的后继者。他的弟子遍及海内外，桃李满天下。1986年，张君秋应李瑞环邀请，赴天津参加天津市青年京剧团"百日集训"工作。1990年底，张君秋应邀赴美国讲学，被授予"人文学"荣誉博士学位，并获得"终身艺术成就奖"。1994年，张君秋接受李瑞环的委托，担任《中国京剧音配像精粹》总顾问。他与京剧界诸多名家一起，充分发挥了艺术造诣精湛、舞台经验丰富的优势，满腔热情地投入到这项对于京剧艺术具有深远意义和十分复杂艰巨的文化工程之中，在近三年的时间里，完成了中国京剧多种流派剧目音配像120部，并为今后的音配像工作奠定了坚实的基础。

张君秋主演的《打渔杀家》《玉堂春》《游龙戏凤》《望江亭》《秦香莲》已摄制成京剧舞台艺术影片，著有《张君秋戏剧散论》。

Biography

Original name: Teng Jia-hong. Ancestral home: Dan Tu, Jiang-su Province. Zhang Jun-qiu was born on October 14th, 1920 (September 3rd, according to the lunar calendar). His father is named Teng Lian-fang, mother named Zhang Xiu-qin, who was a Ching Yi performer of Hebei Clapper opera. Under the influence of his mother, he became quite enthusiastic about drama art. He became the prentice of Li Ling-feng and started learning to play the role of Ching Yi. He made his debut in 1936, and performed in the troupes of Lei Xi-fu, Wang You-chen, Meng Xiao-dong, Ma Lian-liang, Tan Fu-ying respectively. He acquired a national reputation when he was 20 for his handsomeness and his gift. He founded Qian He Troupe in 1942. He also took Wang Yao-qing, Shang Xiao-yun, Mei Lan-fang and Cheng Yan-qiu as his teachers, carefully studied the essence of different schools and inherited the great experience of former Peking Opera artists. He made initial innovative breakthrough in some newly produced plays such as *Double Roosts of Phoenix* and *A Gentle Companion*, etc. In 1948, he flied to Hong Kong with Ma Lian-liang and Yu Zhen-fei to make opera-style films and were trapped there due to wars. With the help of Premier Zhou En-lai, he successfully returned to mainland and joined the Central South Peking Opera Troupe in October 1951. He established the third branch of Beijing Peking Opera Troupe in Beijing in 1952. In 1957, Zhang Jun-qiu, Ma Lian-liang, Tan Fu-ying and Qiu Sheng-rong jointly established Peking Opera Troupe of Beijing.

His most successful period started from mid 1950s to mid 1960s. He successfully inherited the great accomplishments of Mei, Shang, Cheng and Xun. He evolved a unique style of Zhang School by borrowing other schools' special features to combine with his own advantages. On the principle of "Discard the dross and select the essential", he performed a lot of traditional plays: *Liu Lan Zhi* (former name: *Peacocks Fly South East*), *Miss Su San Goes to Trail*, *The Match of Spring and Autumn*, *Princess of Yin ping*, *Da Bao Guo*, *A Visit to the Tomb of Emperor*, *Entering the Palace for the Second Time*, *High-Spirited Horses with Red Long Hair*, *Si Lang Visits His Mother*, *Jin Shan Buddhist Temple*, *Broken Bridge*, and *Lei Feng Pagoda* and further modified *A Gentle Companion*, which gave all of these plays new faces. Moreover, he also performed a batch of Peking Opera historical and modern plays: for example, *Liu Lan Zhi*, *Legend of Color Temple*, *Concubine Zhen*, *Riverside Pavilion*, *The West Chamber*, *A Meeting of Poets*, *The Story in the Palace of Chu*, *Qin Xiang Lian*, *Match Made by Scholar Number One*, *Qiu Jin*, *The Orphan of the Zhao Family*, *Prosperity*, and made them become popular representative plays of Zhang School. In these plays, he displayed Chinese women's intelligence and courage in fighting against the evil forces of old society and molded many vivid stage figures through his unique and natural performances and remarkable voice and expression. His voice was sweet and resonant; his acting was exquisite. The expression in his eyes and the gestures all conveyed the characters' different frames of mind. He was of martial bearing on the stage with beautiful uniform motion and quick and steady movement gestures. In aria, he made full use of his inborn gift of sweet and mellow voice to create many tunes. He paid special attention to the feelings of characters, scrupulously studied and absorbed the features of different schools and fully displayed his singing "soft, charming, crisp, juicy", thus forming a gentle, sweet, energetic and fresh style. His choices of make-up, colors and types of costumes to match with the status and situation of different characters strongly backed up his skillful performances, thus making the roles he played vivid, natural, dignified, and graceful.

All of his innovations were full of strong era breath, which added charm to Peking Opera and enabled his performance to be vivid, expressive and popular among Peking Opera fans. His achievements were unanimously praised by many of his famous counterparts. The formation and spread of the art of Zhang School has exerted profound influence on Dan role (female role) and even the whole Peking Opera art. It also served as an important mark of the glorious achievement that Peking Opera has made in new China.

Despite severe physical and mental tortures in the decade of the Cultural Revolution, Zhang Jun-qiu's faith in communism remained unswerving. His life was back on track and actively took part in social activities such as becoming the vice president of China Traditional Opera Institute after the breakdown of "Gang of Four". He became a member of CPC (Communist Party of China) with honor in June 1981. He was elected the member of the 5th National Committee of the Chinese People's Political Consultative. Later, he was chosen as the Standing Committee member of the 6th, 7th and 8th National Committee of the Chinese People's Political Consultative; as Vice-chairman of the 4th and 5th National Literature and Art Association; as Vice-chairman of National Association of Drama; as the honorary president of Chinese Peking Opera Art Fund.

He embraced highly sense of responsibility in vitalizing Peking Opera in his old age. He made great contributions and his role was indispensable. Facing with the ruins, a scarcity of Peking Opera actors, actresses and plays, resulted from the 10-year Cultural Revolution, he resolutely decided to shift the focus of his work to the cultivation of young Peking Opera performers. As the vice president of China Traditional Opera Institute, he should be credited with much of the progress. Apart from completing his task of teaching splendidly, he also devoted himself to cultivation of young Peking Opera performers. He has students in every nook and cranny of the world. In 1986, at the invitation of Li Rui-huan, mayor of Tianjin municipality, he assumed the task of training the performers of Tianjin Young Peking Opera Troupe one hundred days. In 1990, he was invited to lecture in the United States and was entitled honorary Humanity doctorate as well as the prize for "lifelong achievement in art". In 1994, Li Rui-huan entrusted Zhang Jun-qiu with the task of being the senior counselor of the "Peking Opera Audio-videotaped Classics". Together with many other famous Peking Opera experts, he fully displayed their advantages in artistic attainments and rich stage experiences and enthusiastically dedicated himself to this complex cultural project, which has profound influence on the development of Peking Opera. They succeeded in completing the project of audio-videotaping 120 Peking Opera plays of different schools in 3 years, which laid a solid foundation for the audio-videotaping project in the future.

The operas which Zhang Jun-qiu acted as leading roles such as *The Fishman's Revenge, Spring of Jade Hall, Prince and the Showgirl, Riverside Pavilion, Qin Xiang-lian* have been made into Peking Opera stage art films . He also wrote a book named "Viewpoints on Opera--Zhang Jun-qiu".

毛泽东主席接见京剧界人士。左起张君秋、裘盛戎、石少华、谭富英、毛泽东、谭元寿、马长礼
Chair man Mao met with celebrities in the walks of Peking Opera. From left: Zhang Jun-qiu, Qiu Sheng-rong, Shi Shao-hua, Tan Fu-ying, Mao Ze-dong, Tan Yuan-shou, Ma Chang-li.

中央领导同张君秋

周恩来总理接见张君秋

Premier Zhou En-lai met with Zhang Jun-qiu.

张君秋陪同邓小平、李先念同志观看京剧《红灯照》,演出后一起上台接见演员

Zhang Jun-qiu escorted Comrade Deng Xiao-ping and Comrade Li Xian-nian to watch Peking Opera *Legend of Red Lantern*, and then had photos taken with performers on the stage after the performance.

江泽民、万里、乔石、李瑞环同志在"纪念徽班晋京二百周年"活动开幕式上，观看张君秋等演出的《龙凤呈祥》后，合影留念

Group photo with Comrade Jiang Ze-min, Comrade Wan Li, Comrade Qiao Shi and Comrade Li Rui-huan after they watched the performance of *Prosperity Brought by the Dragon and the Phoenix* in the opening ceremony in memory of the 200th Anniversary of Anhui Troupe's Entering into Beijing.

李瑞环同志会见张君秋
Comrade Li Rui-huan met with Zhang Jun-qiu.

张君秋艺术形象

Zhang Jun-qiu's Artistic Images

《五花洞》中饰潘金莲

In *Cave of Five Flowers* as Pan Jin-lian.

《十三妹》中饰何玉凤
In *Sister Thirteen* as He Yu-feng.

《虹霓关》中饰丫鬟

In *Hong Ni Pass* as servant girl.

《女起解》中饰苏三，萧长华饰崇公道
In *Miss Su San Goes to Trial* as Su San, Xiao Chang-hua as Chong Gong-dao.

《红拂传》中饰张凌华

In *Legend of Hong Fu* as Zhang Ling-hua.

《御碑亭》中饰孟月华

In *The Imperial Stele Pavilion* as Meng Yue-hua.

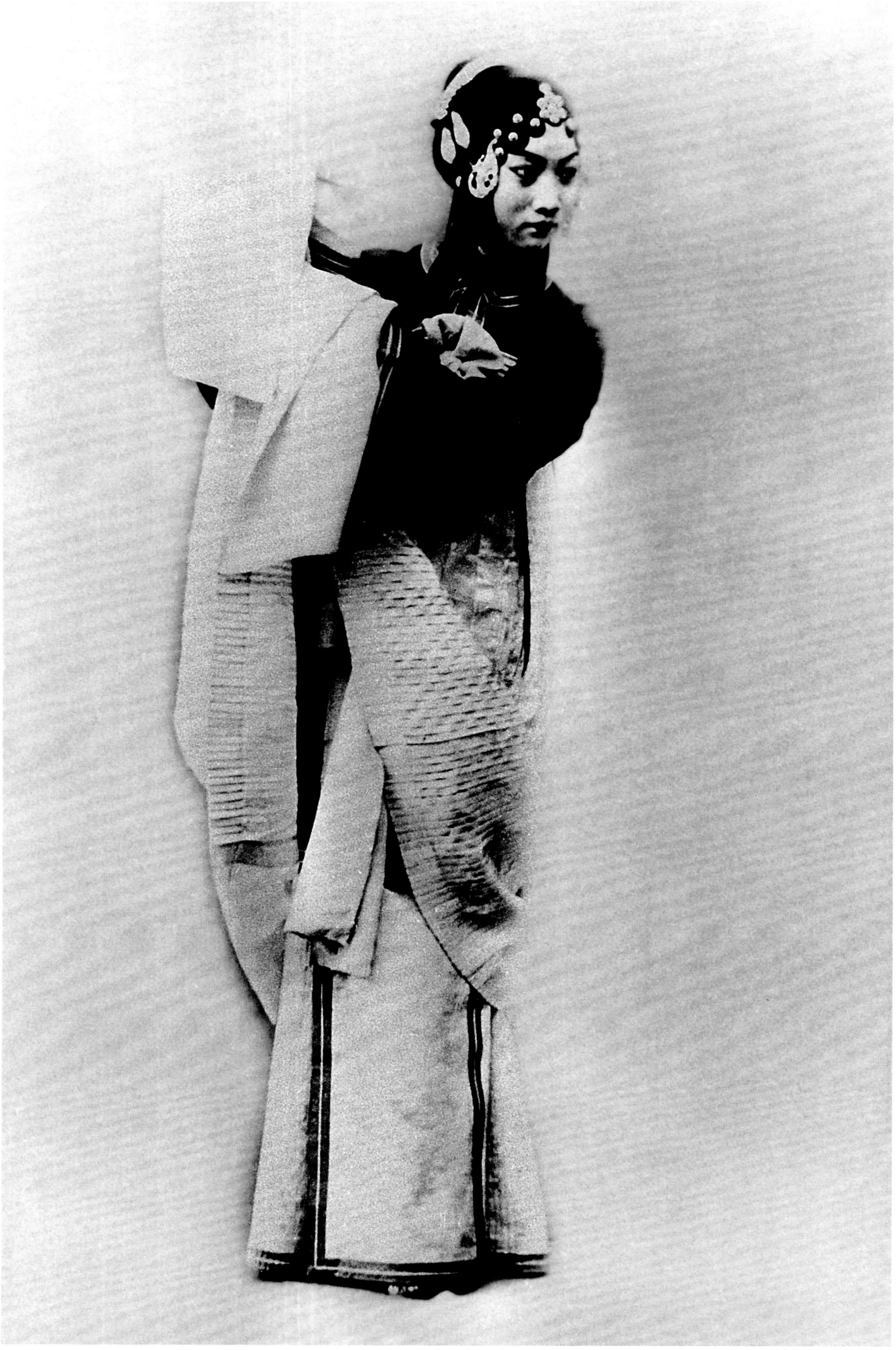

《审头刺汤》中饰雪艳

In *Identifying the Head and Stabbing Tang* as Xue Yan.

《梅龙镇》中饰李凤姐,马连良饰正德皇帝

In *Meilong Town* as Sister Li Feng, Ma Lian-liang as Emperor Zheng De.

《霸王别姬》中饰虞姬

In *Farewell My Concubine* as Concubine Yu.

《回荆州》中饰孙尚香

In *Liu Bei Returns to JingZhou* as Sun Shang-xiang.

《四郎探母》中饰铁镜公主
In *Si Lang Visits His Mother* as Tie Jing Princess.

《金山寺、断桥、雷峰塔》中饰白素贞

In *Temple in Gold Mountain, The Broken Bridge and Lei Feng Pagoda* as Bai Su-zhen.

《凤还巢》中饰程雪娥

In *The Phoenix Returns to Its Nest* as Cheng Xue-er.

《怜香伴》中饰崔笺云
In *A Gentle Companion* as Cui Jian-yun.

《彩楼记》中饰刘翠屏

In *The Legend of Color Building* as Liu Cui-ping.

《望江亭》中饰谭记儿

In *Riverside Pavilion* as Tan Ji-er.

《状元媒》中饰柴郡主

In *Match Made by Scholar Number One* as Chai Jun-zhu.

《西厢记》中饰崔莺莺
In *The West Chamber* as Cui Ying-ying.

《诗文会》中饰车静芳

In *A Meeting of Poets* as Che Jing-fang.

《秋瑾》中饰秋瑾
In *Qiu Jin* as Qiu Jin.

《秦香莲》中饰秦香莲

In *Qin Xiang Lian* as Qin Xiang-lian.

《赵氏孤儿》中饰庄姬

In *Orphan of Zhao Family* as Concubine Zhuang.

《龙凤呈祥》中饰孙尚香

In *Prosperity Brought by the Dragon and the Phoenix* as Sun Shang-xiang.

1920年，张君秋出生在北京的一个平民家庭里。

张君秋在母亲、河北梆子青衣演员张秀琴的熏陶下，热爱戏曲艺术。

看到母亲操劳辛苦，他向母亲提出学戏的要求。

1933年，拜师李凌枫，刻苦学艺。

1936年，张君秋初登舞台，

以俊美的扮相、甜亮的嗓音赢得了观众的青睐，

开始了搭班演戏的舞台生涯。

In 1920, Zhang Jun-qiu was born in a family of ordinary people in Beijing. Under the influence of his mother who was a clapper opera performer, he became quite enthusiastic about drama art. In 1933, he became the prentice of Li Ling-feng. He made his debut in 1936 when his handsomeness and sweet voice won the favors of the viewers, which was the beginning of his stage life.

Peking Opera Master ZHANG JUNQIU

STUDY 求学篇

苦难童年 Miserable Childhood　**拜师学艺** Taking a Master to Learn a Craft
崭露头角 Beginning to Show His Brilliant Talents

苦难童年 Miserable Childhood

张君秋幼时家境清贫，父亲流落在外，随母亲张秀琴住在外祖母家里。张秀琴是一位河北梆子青衣演员，一家七口人靠她一人在外演戏维持生活。张君秋小时候长得清秀，母亲把他当成女孩子妆扮。上了一段私塾和平民小学，因家庭经济拮据而辍学。十来岁的时候，开始随母亲到保定、张家口一带演出，渐渐对戏曲发生了浓厚的兴趣。看到母亲为养家昼夜操劳，日渐消瘦，他向母亲提出了学戏的要求。

His family led an impoverished life in his childhood. He lived in his grandmother's home with his mother and no one knew his father's whereabouts. Because of his delicate appearance, his mother dressed him as a girl. He once studied in private school and public school for some time before dropping out for poverty. He began to perform with his mother in Baoding and Zhang Jiakou at about 10 and he gradually took to drama. Having seen his hard-working mother become emaciated day after day, he told his mother that he wanted to learn opera in order to make a living.

童年（1921）
Childhood (1921).

同母亲张秀琴（1936）
Together with his mother Zhang Xiu-qin(1936).

张君秋幼时与家人合影

前右坐藤椅者为张君秋，时年六岁。其身后为张母张秀琴。中坐老人为张之外婆，后排左起第一人为张之舅母（何顺信之岳母）。前排右起第一人为张之兄张君杰，第二人为张之表妹（何顺信之妻），其他儿童均为张之表兄妹

A photo with family members in his childhood

Front row on the right, Zhang Jun-qiu sat on the ratten chair, six years old; mother Zhang Xiu-qin was behind him; grandmother sat in the middle; back row first left zhang's aunt (mother-in-law of He Shun-xin). Front row first right, brother Zhang Jun-jie; second right Zhang's cousin (He Shun-xin's wife), the rest are zhang's cousins.

拜师学艺 Taking a Master to Learn a Craft

1933年，张君秋立关书，拜师李凌枫学习京剧青衣艺术，开始了艰苦的学艺生涯。他在《我的艺术道路》一文中记述了自己幼时练功的情景："在师傅家学戏、排戏，多是在院子里。多冷的天也是这样：排戏之前脱了小棉袄，先踢踢腿，活动一下身体，然后拉开架势跑一通圆场，直跑得满身大汗为止，这才给拉身段。拉起身段来，就不像跑圆场的运动量那样大了，可在院子里一站，长时间不动，身上的汗还没落，西北风一吹，就显得格外冷。即便如此，我也绝不披上小棉袄，惟恐师傅嫌我吃不了苦。好不容易学了戏，如果让师傅送回家不教我了，那可就失去了学戏的机会了。我小时候，家里生活苦，身体缺营养，很单薄，可多冷的天我也得忍着，心里想，既然我说过'什么样的苦我也能吃'，那么，我就得说到做到，这样一来才能学戏呀！到了三伏天，多热的天也照样练功，一天到晚，全身上下汗水淋淋，腰上勒的板带没有干的时候，晚上解开板带挂起来吹吹风，第二天早晨没干又得给勒上。"由于张君秋天资聪颖，又肯刻苦练功，学戏学得很快。张君秋的聪慧、刻苦与好学受到了李凌枫的师傅王瑶卿的赏识，王瑶卿开始向他隔代传艺。

In 1993, he began his arduous apprentice life in learning Ching Yi under the guidance of Li Ling-feng. He described how he was trained in his article "My Art Road": most of the time I was trained in my master's courtyard, even in winter; I must take off the coat before rehearsal and did some warming-up exercises such as kicking and running to prepare for body-stretching until I was soaked with sweat. The body-stretching part was not as exhausting as running. However, I shivered all over while standing still for a long time with shirt soaked in sweat and facing the chilly wind. But I wouldn't put on my coat for fear that the master might think that I am not tough enough for hardships and send me back home. I was skinny and suffered from malnutrition for poverty. I was thinking that I mustn't give up however chilly the weather might be. I once talked to myself: I can tolerate any hardships and I can make it. There was no exception even in the three hottest periods of a year. From dawn to dark I perspired all over. The belt around my waist was soaked with sweat all the time except the time I went to sleep when it could be hung to dry, and it would be put on again when it was still wet. "Being gifted, intelligent and diligent, he was appreciated by his master's master Wang Yao-qing, who began to take Zhang Jun-qiu together as his student.

同师傅李凌枫（1936）
李凌枫，字缉之，江苏嘉定人，原学医，爱好京剧，私淑程派，后弃医"下海"，拜王瑶卿为师。

Together with master Li Ling-feng(1936)
Li Ling-feng, also known as Ji Yi-zhi; Ancestral home: Jia Ding, Jiang-su Province. He used to be a doctor, but showed great affection for Peking Opera, especially Cheng School. Later, he transfer-red himself to become a Peking Opera performer, with Wang Yao-qing as the master.

① 在陶然亭湖边
On the lakeside of Tao Ran Pavilion.

② ③ 张君秋学艺期间，坚持每天去陶然亭湖边喊嗓
During Zhang Jun-qiu's learning period, he kept on practicing his throat along Tao Ran Ting Lake every morning.

①

②

③

求学篇

拜师学艺

　　王瑶卿，字雅庭，号菊痴，艺名瑶卿，晚年更名瑶青。祖籍江苏清江，生于北京。唱、念、做、打，全面发展，改变了以往旦角表演中只攻一端的旧规，打破了过去京剧舞台上仅生行领衔的局面，是京剧旦角艺术的革新开拓者。46岁时因"塌中"息影舞台，专门致力于培育后学。梅兰芳、程砚秋、荀慧生、尚小云等四大名旦多请益于他。张君秋拜师李凌枫后，因其资质聪颖，遂得王瑶卿赏识，因而对张君秋隔代相授。

Wang Yao-qing, also known as Ya Ting, respectfully addressed as Ju Chi, with Yao-qing as his stage name. Ancestral home: Qing Jiang , Jiang-su Province. Born in Beijing, he was the pioneer in innovating the role of Dan in Peking Opera. He made the role of Dan develop in an all-round way, such as singing, dialogue, acting and martial arts, which enabled Dan (female roles) to become another leading part on the stage besides the role of Sheng (male roles). When he was 46, he retired from the stage because of hoarseness. Then he spent the rest of his life in nurturing young generations. It was Wang Yao-qing who enriched the art of performing the Dan roles, taking the Peking Opera a step forward. Under his instruction and guidance appeared the four eminent schools of Dan roles: those of Mei Lan-fang, Shang Xiao-yun, Cheng Yan-qiu and Xun Hui-sheng. After Zhang Jun-qiu became Li Ling-feng's prentice, his talents and intelligence were greatly appreciated by Wang Yao-qing who was Li Ling-feng's master. Then Wang Yao-qing also became Zhang Jun-qiu's master.

崭露头角 Beginning to Show His Brilliant Talents

1936年初,张君秋第一次登台演出《女起解》,引起了观众的注目。之后他陆续在雷喜福、王又宸、孟小冬、谭富英、马连良等班社搭班,相继在北京、天津、上海、山东等地演出,红遍大江南北。

His debut in *Miss Su San Goes to Trial* in 1936 won him great reputation. His successive performances in the troupes of Lei Xi-fu, Wang You-chen, Meng Xiao-dong, Tan Fu-ying and Ma Lian-liang in Beijing, Tianjin, Shanghai and Shandong won him a nationwide popularity.

张君秋(1936)
Zhang Jun-qiu (1936).

①

②

③

①《女起解》中饰苏三,萧长华饰崇公道（1938）
In *Miss Su San Goes to Trial* as Su San, Xiao Chang-hua as Chong Gong-dao(1938).

②《御碑亭》中饰孟月华（1937）
In *The Imperial Stele Pavilion* as Meng Yue-hua(1937).

③《奇双会》中饰李桂枝，叶盛兰饰赵宠
In *Selling Horse* as Li Gui-zhi, Ye Sheng-Lan as Zhao Chong.

① 《贵妃醉酒》中饰杨玉环（1937）
In *Drunken Concubine* as Yang Yu-huan (1937).

② 《四郎探母》中饰铁镜公主（1937）
In *Si Lang Visits His Mother* as Tie Jing Princess (1937).

① 1937年6月8日与马连良在上海赈灾义演的海报
The poster of his and Ma Lian-liang's performance in Shanghai for people in disaster-stricken areas, June 8th, 1937.

② 1937年5月1日与马连良在上海演出的海报
The poster of his and Ma Lian-liang's performance in Shanghai, May 1st, 1937.

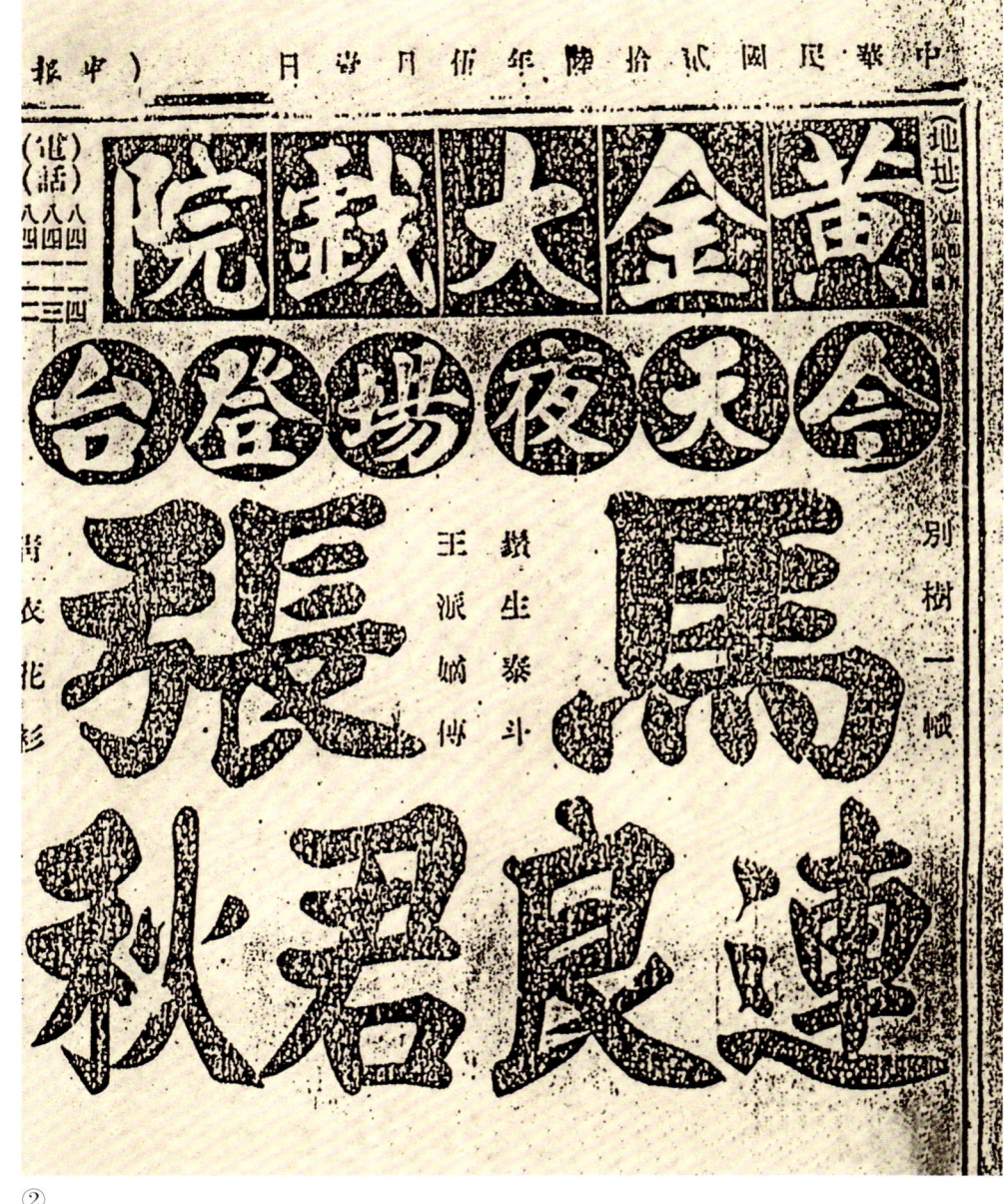

① 《桑园会》中饰罗敷,马连良饰秋胡(1938)
In *Meeting in Mulberry Garden* as Luo Fu, Ma Lian-liang as Qiu Hu (1938).

② 《打渔杀家》中饰萧桂英,马连良饰萧恩(1938)
In *The Fisherman's Revenge* as Xiao Gui-ying, Ma Lian-liang as Xiao En (1938).

《梅龙镇》中饰李凤姐,谭富英饰正德皇帝(1939)
In *Meilong Town* as Sister Li Feng, Tan Fu-ying as Emperor Zheng De(1939).

①《五花洞》中饰潘金莲（1938）
In *Cave of Five Flowers* as Pan Jin-lian(1938).

②《断桥》中饰白素贞（1938）
In *Broken Bridge* as Bai Su-zhen(1938).

求学篇

崭露头角

①

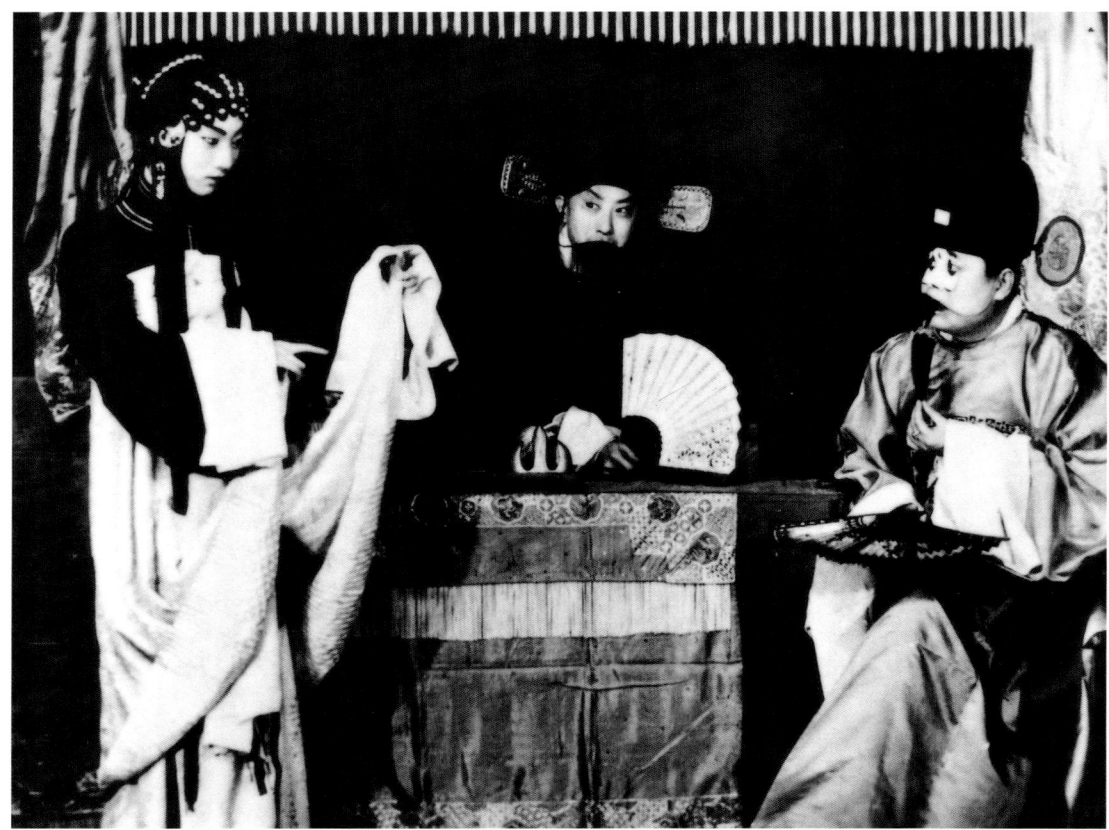
②

③

①张君秋（1938）
Zhang Jun-qiu (1938).

②《审头刺汤》中饰雪艳，马连良饰陆炳，马富禄饰汤勤（1938）
In *Shen Tou Ci Tang* as Xue Yan, Ma Lian-liang as Lu Bing, Ma Fu-lu as Tang Qin (1938).

③《审头刺汤》中饰雪艳（1938）
In *Shen Tou Ci Tang* as Xue Yan (1938).

①

②

③

①《十三妹》中饰何玉凤（1938）
In *Sister Thirteen* as He Yu-feng (1938).

②《十三妹》中饰何玉凤（1938）
In *Sister Thirteen* as He Yu-feng (1938).

③《能仁寺》中饰张金凤（1939）
In *Neng Ren Temple* as Zhang Jin-feng (1939).

孟小冬張君秋御碑亭劇照

孟小冬之劇照，向稱名貴，以其自加珍惜，不輕攝亦不輕爲人攝也。此幀乃上月三十日攝於開明戲院者，是夕小冬與張君秋演御碑亭。小冬飾王有道，君秋飾孟月華，一則古樸簡淨之中，神完氣足，朗如秋月，一則雍容華貴，雅潔端莊之態，艷似春花。尤以小冬在當時見愚爲之攝影，因富交誼，屹立未稍移動。其眉目頰頰，與乃師余叔岩之探母等像幾可鑑鯉莫辨。惜乎燈光太強，不適攝影，否則更當有如襃鄂毛髮颯爽生姿矣。

（幼三攝贈並識）

①《御碑亭》中飾孟月华，孟小冬饰王有道
In *The Imperial Stele Pavilion* as Meng Yue-hua, Meng Xiao-dong as Wang You-dao.

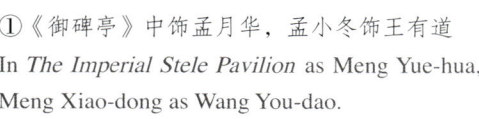

②《汾河湾》中饰柳迎春（1939）
In *Bay of Fen River* as Liu Ying-chun (1939).

《二进宫》中饰李艳妃，谭富英饰杨波，王泉奎饰徐延昭（1938）
In *Entering the Palace for the Second Time* as Li Yan-fei, Tan Fu-ying as Yang Bo, Wang Quan-kui as Xu Yan-zhao (1938).

张君秋（1938）
Zhang Jun-qiu (1938).

1936年，张君秋在王瑶卿的严格要求下，坚持了六年的搭班生涯。
他先后与雷喜福、王又宸、孟小冬、谭富英、马连良等
不同流派的老生演员合作，
又先后得到尚小云、梅兰芳、程砚秋的教益，
博采众长，艺事愈进，戏路愈宽，积累了丰富的舞台经验。
1942年，张君秋自组"谦和社"，声誉鹊起。
1948年，同马连良、俞振飞赴香港演出，因战事频仍，留居香港。

Under the Arequest of Wang Yao-qing, he kept on performing in different troupes for 6 years, when he had the chances to cooperate with many Laosheng performers such as Lei Xi-fu, Wang You-chen, Meng Xiao-dong, Tan Fu-ying and Ma Lian-liang. He was later fortunately instructed by Shang Xiao-yun, Mei Lan-fang and Cheng Yan-qiu and enriched his stage experiences by absorbing the advantages of various schools. In 1948, with Ma Lian-liang and Yu Zhen-fei, he flew to Hong Kong where they were trapped because of wars.

PURSUIT 求索篇

博采众长 Learning from Others **自组班社** The Establishment of His Own Troupe
香港之旅 Tour in Hong Kong

博采众长 Learning from Others

从1936年初次登台演出到1942年自组"谦和社",张君秋经过了六年的搭班演出生涯。其间,《立言画刊》组织观众推选"四小名旦",张君秋名列其中。在该刊请他填写的表格栏目中有这样一个提问:"你最推崇的名家是谁?"他填写为"凡在艺术上有成就者,均是我学习的师长"。在他搭班演出的过程中,京剧界对他组班自己挑头牌当主演的呼声很大,但他不为之所动,而是听从了王瑶卿的告诫"要成好角,不要当好角",没有受虚名的干扰,脚踏实地在搭班生涯中一边实践,一边学习,广泛向阎岚秋(九阵风)、冯子和、张彩林、朱桂芳、姜玉珮、郑传鉴、朱传茗等请教,不断提高自己的艺术水平。王瑶卿针对同张君秋合作的不同老生演员的戏路子,为他加工指点了大量的生、旦传统对儿戏,为张君秋的旦角艺术打下了牢固的基础,使他在同雷喜福、王又宸、孟小冬、谭富英、马连良等不同流派艺术演出实践中,熟悉了不同的戏路,增强了艺术表现力,积累了丰富的艺术创作经验。在他初登舞台之时,便受到尚小云的赏识,主动提出为张君秋说戏。张君秋向尚小云学习了尚派剧目《春秋配》、《御碑亭》、《汉明妃》等,并随尚小云在长庆社同台演出《乾坤福寿镜》、《九曲黄河阵》、《牛郎织女》等剧目。1937年,张君秋搭马连良"扶风社"班在上海演出期间,拜师梅兰芳,学习了《凤还巢》、《生死恨》、《霸王别姬》、《贵妃醉酒》、《奇双会》等梅派剧目。1941年,张君秋又得到程砚秋的热情指点,学习了程派剧目《贺后骂殿》、《牧羊卷》、《红拂传》、《六月雪》等。他遵从王瑶卿、梅兰芳、程砚秋等师长的告诫,不仅认真学好各派艺术家的剧目,而且在演出实践中注意发挥自己的艺术特长,开始了创新的探索。

From his debut in 1936 to 1942 when he founded Qian He Troupe, he experienced 6 years of performing in different troupes. In 1940, viewers organized by *Li Yan Illustrated* selected Zhang Jun-qiu as one of the "Four Junior Great Female Role Players". *Li Yan Illustrated* asked him to fill a form in which there was a question: "Who is your most respected master?" He answered, "Anyone who has his own achievements can be my teacher." From 1936 to 1942, many people in the walks of Peking Opera claimed that Zhang Jun-qiu was full-fledged enough to form his own troupe, but he was clear-minded and had the knowledge of himself. Instead of being self-important, he bore in mind what Wang Yao-qing told him: to be a good performer rather than play the good roles only, and freed himself from being affected the undeserved reputation. He continued to practice and study in a conscientious and reliable manner. He kept on enhancing his proficiency by seeking advice from Yan Lan-qiu, Feng Zi-he, Zhang Cai-lin, Zhu Gui-fang, Jiang Yu-pei, Zheng Chuan-jian and Zhu Chuan-ming. Based on the character type of different Laosheng actors cooperating with Zhang Jun-qiu, Wang Yao-qing revised a large number of traditional pair performances of Sheng and Dan roles, all of which not only laid a solid foundation for Zhang Jun-qiu's performance in Dan roles, but also enabled him to be familiarized with different character types while he was cooperating with Lei Xi-fu, Wang You-chen, Meng Xiao-dong, Tan Fu-ying and Ma Lian-liang from different schools of Peking Opera, thus making his performance more expressive and he accumulated more experiences. On his debut, he left a good impression on Shang Xiao-yun, who volunteered to be Zhang's master. Zhang Jun-qiu learned Shang School's representative plays *The Match of Spring and Autumn*, *The Imperial Stele Pavilion*, *Wang Zhao-jun's Marriage*, and performed *Qian Kun Fu Shou Mirror*, *Jiu Qu Yellow River*, *Lantern Herd Boy* and *Spinning Girl* with Shang Xiao-yun in Chang Qing Troupe. In 1937, he performed in Ma Lian-liang's Fu Feng Troupe in Shanghai where he took Mei Lan-fang as his master and learned to play *The Phoenix Returns to Its Nest*, *Farewell between Life and Death*, *Farewell My Concubine*, *The Drunken Concubine* and *Selling Horse*, all of which were the representative plays of Mei School. In 1941, he was instructed by Cheng Yan-qiu and learned Cheng School's representative plays: *Picture of Two Emperors*, *Legend of Zhu Heng*, *Legend of Hong Fu*, *Snow in June*. Bearing in mind the earnest and tireless admonishments of Wang Yao-qing, Mei Lan-fang and Cheng Yan-qiu, he conscientiously studied the representative plays of different schools and realized the importance of displaying his advantages in performance and began his path on innovation.

《御碑亭》中饰孟月华(40年代)
In *The Imperial Stele Pavilion* as Meng Yue-hua(1940s).

① 《樊江关》中饰薛金莲（40年代）
In *Fan Jiang Pass* as Xue Jin-lian(1940s).

② 《樊江关》中饰樊梨花（40年代）
In *Fan Jiang Pass* as Fan Li-hua(1940s).

《四郎探母》中饰铁镜公主,谭富英饰杨延辉(30年代)

In *Si Lang Visits His Mother* as Tie Jing Princess, Tan Fu-ying as Yang Yan-hui(1930s).

① 《摘缨会》中饰许姬，马连良饰楚庄王（1939）
In *Zhai Ying Meeting* as Princess Xu, Ma Lian-liang as King Chu Zhuang (1939).

② 1937年与马连良在"扶风社"合作演出的海报
The poster of his cooperative performance with Ma Lian-liang in Fu Feng Troupe in 1937.

①

③

②

① 《虹霓关》中饰丫鬟（30年代）
In *Hong Ni Pass* as the servant girl(1930s).

② 《虹霓关》中饰东方氏，叶盛兰饰王伯党（30年代）
In *Hong Ni Pass* as Dong Fang-shi, Ye Sheng-lan as Wang Bo-dang(1930s).

③ 《虹霓关》中饰丫鬟，于连泉饰东方氏，叶盛兰饰王伯党（30年代）
In *Hong Ni Pass* as the servant girl, Yu Lian-quan as Dong Fang-shi, Ye Sheng-lan as Wang Bo-dang(1930s).

① "四小名旦"合影。左起：李世芳、毛世来、张君秋、宋德珠（1946）
Photo of the Four Junior Great Female Role Players, namely: Li Shi-fang, Mao Shi-lai, Zhang Jun-qiu, Song De-zhu (1946).

② 1938年12月24日，《立言画刊》关于"四小名旦"的评论文章。该文提出"张君秋今日之红，确乎凌驾一般而上"
On December 24th, 1938, the commentary on the Four Junior Great Female Role Players was published in *Li Yan Illustrated*, saying that his popularity indeed outstripped others.

① 《五花洞》中饰潘金莲
In *Cave of Five Flowers* as Pan Jin-lian.

② 《武家坡》中饰王宝钏
In *Wu Jia Po* as Wang Bao-chuan.

求索篇

博采众长

① 《群英会》中反串周瑜
In *A Gathering of Heroes* Zhang Jun-qiu as a male role Zhou Yu.

② 1939年3月11日,《立言画刊》发表评论文章,标题为"张君秋真天之骄子"
On March 11th, 1939 a commentary entitled "Zhang Jun-qiu, an unusually lucky person" was published in *Li Yan Illustrated*.

①《审头刺汤》中饰雪艳，马富禄饰汤勤（1940）
In *Identifying the Head and Stabbing Tang* as Xue Yan, Ma Fu-lu as Tang Qin (1940).

②《梅龙镇》中饰李凤姐，谭富英饰正德皇帝（30年代）
In *Meilong Town* as Sister Li Feng, Tan Fu-ying as Emperor Zheng De(1930s).

同梅兰芳（左二）、周信芳（右二）、谭小培（右三）在上海聚餐（1938）
Having dinner with Mei Lan-fang (second left), Zhou Xin-fang (second right), Tan Xiao-pei (third right) in ShangHai (1938).

在《游园惊梦》中饰春香,李世芳饰杜丽娘
In *Peony Pavilion* as Chun Xiang, Li Shi-fang as Du Li-niang.

求索篇

博采众长

前排左起：詹世辅、尚富霞、尚长春、尚小云、毛世来。后排左起：毛盛荣、张君秋、李世芳、袁世海、阎世善

From row left: Zhan Shi-fu, Shang Fu-xia, Shang Chang-chun, Shang Xiao-yun, Mao Shi-lai. Back row left: Mao Sheng-rong, Zhang Jun-qiu, Li Shi-fang, Yuan Shi-hai, Yan Shi-shan.

① 《汾河湾》中饰柳迎春（40年代）
In *Bay of Fen River* as Liu Ying-chun(1940s).

② 《四郎探母》中饰铁镜公主（40年代）
In *Si Lang Visits His Mother* as Princess Tie Jing(1940s).

《红拂传》中饰张凌华（1941）

In *Legend of Hong Fu* as Zhang Ling-hua(1941).

自组班社　The Establishment of His Own Troupe

　　1942年张君秋自挂头牌，组成"谦和社"，其岳父、北平梨园公会会长赵砚奎任社长。此时，他已积累了大量的演出剧目。组班之后，王瑶卿又为他演出的折子戏增加了头尾，如《三娘教子》加头尾成为全部《王春娥》，《梅龙镇》加头尾成为全部《骊珠恨》，《祭江》加头尾成为全部《孙尚香》，《断桥》加头尾，成为全部《金山寺、断桥、雷峰塔》等，丰富了他的演出剧目。"谦和社"的演出轰动了京、津、沪。当时的报刊载文称："张君秋自组'谦和社'后，名誉地位更进一步。《红拂传》之演出，益征其广揽各派之长，戏路愈宽矣！君秋所采方法，融合梅、尚、程三派……名伶之成名，岂偶然哉！"张君秋还排演了一些新剧目，如《凤双栖》、《奇烈记》、《怜香伴》、《银屏公主》。在这些剧目的排演中，张君秋在唱腔演唱上作了创新尝试，积累了一些经验。

　　In 1942, as a leading member, he founded Qian He Troupe with his father-in-law Zhao Yan-kui, chairman of The Operatic Circle in Beijing, as the head. At that time, he accumulated a large amount of experience in performance. Moreover, Wang Yao-qing helped to add the beginning part and the ending part for the arias he performed, for example, adding beginning part and ending part for *The Third Mistress Brings Up the Son* to make a whole opera *Wang Chun E*, adding the beginning part and ending part for *Mei Long Town* to make a whole opera *Hatred of Li Zhu*, adding the beginning part and ending part for *Sacrificing at the Riverside* to make a whole opera *Sun Shang Xiang*, adding the beginning part and ending part for *Broken Bridge* to make a whole opera *Jin Shan Buddhist Temple, Broken Bridge* and *Lei Feng Pagoda*, thus enriching his performing plays. The performances presented by Qian He Troupe caused a sensation in Beijing, Tianjin and Shanghai. Reports in the newspaper at that time claimed that Zhang Jun-qiu's reputation and status stepped onto a new stage after the performance of Qian He Troupe. His performance in *Legend of Hong Fu* embodied the advantages of different schools and he became suitable to more character types. It is no surprise for his success because his performance integrated the advantages of Mei Lan-fang, Shang Xiao-yun and Cheng Yan-qiu. He also performed some new plays, such as *Double Roosts of Phoenix, Legend of Warriors, A Gentle Companion, Princess Yin Ping*, in which he presented originality in aria and gained some experiences.

张君秋（1943）
Zhang Jun-qiu(1943).

求索篇
自组班社

40年代初报刊有关张君秋组班的报道。其中报道了谦和社首场演出的盛况,并说:"从此谦和社莫定江山矣。"

News on Zhang Jun-qiu's founding Qian He Troupe in the 1940s, among which the grand debut of Qian He Troupe was reported. It said that Qian He Troupe was going to be prosperous.

① 谦和社社长赵砚奎
Zhao Yan-kui, head of Qian He Troupe.

② 谦和社演出戏单
The performance list of Qian He Troupe.

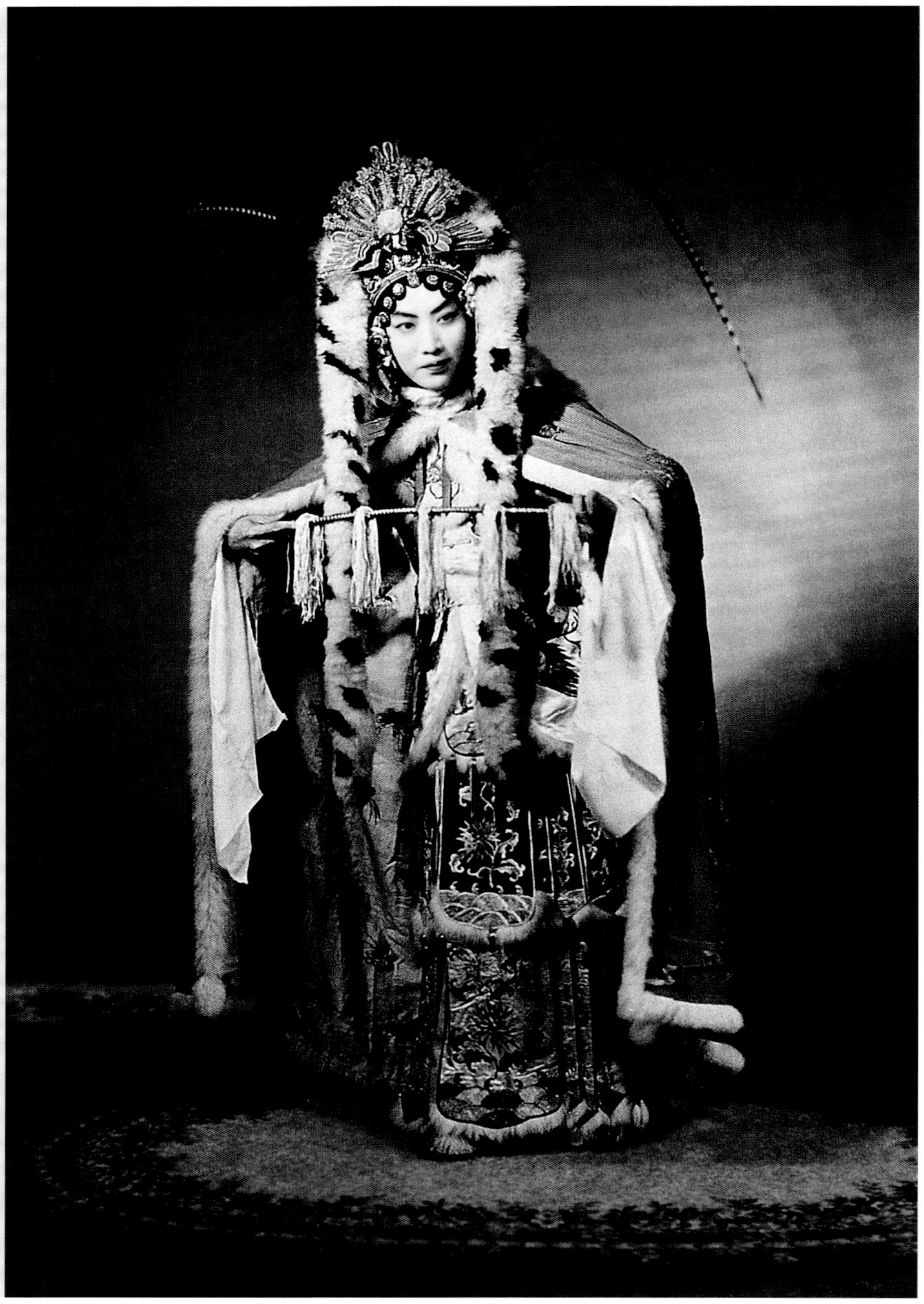

①

②

①②《汉明妃》中饰王昭君（40年代）
In *Wang Zhao-jun's Marriage* as Wang Zhao-jun (1940s).

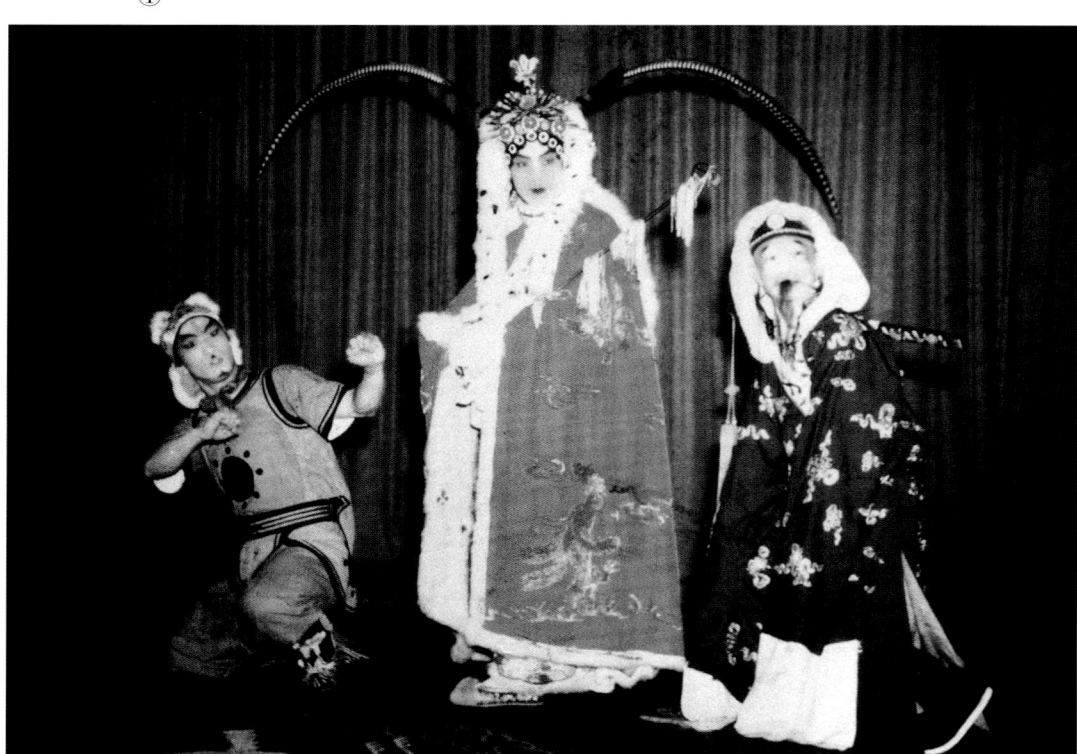

求索篇

自组班社

①

②

① 程砚秋
Cheng Yan-qiu.

②《红拂传》中饰张凌华（1947）
In *Legend of Hong Fu* as Zhang Ling-hua (1947).

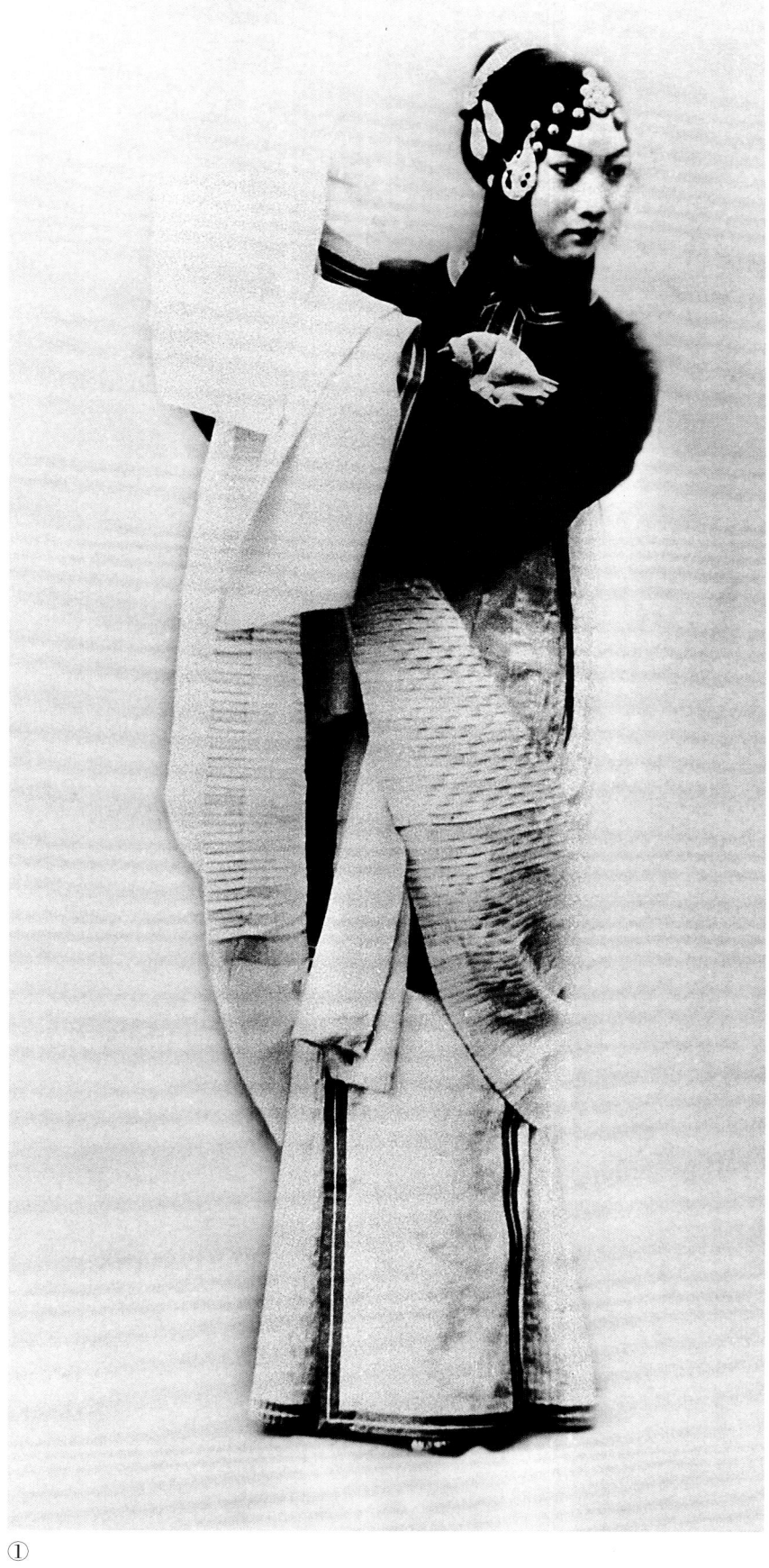

① 《审头刺汤》中饰雪艳（1947）

In *Identifying the Head and Stabbing Tang* as Xue Yan (1947).

② 《霸王别姬》中饰虞姬

In *Farewell My Concubine* as Concubine Yu.

求索篇

自组班社

① 同夫人吴励箴女士（1944）
Together with his wife Ms Wu Li-zhen (1944).

② 三代同堂　左起：张学津、张学沄、张秀琴、张学聪、张学浩、张君秋、张学华、张学江、吴励箴
Three generations under the same roof, from left: Zhang Xue-jin, Zhang Xue-yun, Zhang Xiu-qin, Zhang Xue-cong, Zhang Xue-hao, Zhang Jun-qiu, Zhang Xue-hua, Zhang Xue-jiang, Wu Li-zhen.

① 1946年在上海。由左至右，第一排：高玉倩、于连泉、谭小培、杨宝森、袁世海；第二排：谭富英、李少春、李多奎、马富禄；第三排：张君秋、陈大濩、叶盛章、阎世善、万子和、苗胜春；第四排：（左不详）右赵荣琛。
In Shanghai in 1946. From left, first row: Gao Yu-qian, Yu Lian-quan, Tan Xiao-pei, Yang Bao-sen, Yuan Shi-hai; second row, Tan Fu-ying, Li Shao-chun, Li Duo-kui, Ma Fu-lu; third row, Zhang Jun-qiu, Chen Da-huo, Ye Sheng-zhang, Wan Z i-he, Miao Sheng-chun; fourth row, (the left one unknown) the right one was Zhao Rong-chen.

② 同荀慧生、李世芳等在一起（1941）
Together with Xun Hui-sheng and Li Shi-fang(1941).

③ 张君秋（1947）
Zhang Jun-qiu (1947).

同梅兰芳等在上海国际饭店（1947）
Together with Mei Lan-fang in Shanghai International Hotel (1947).

香港之旅   Tour in Hong Kong

1948年，张君秋应邀与马连良、俞振飞至香港演出，并应香港胜利影片公司的邀请，拍摄了戏曲影片《打渔杀家》、《梅龙镇》（与马连良合作）、《玉堂春》（与俞振飞合作）。因战事阻隔，留居香港。

In 1948, he, together with Ma Lian-liang and Yu Zhen-fei, at the invitation of Hong Kong Victory Film Company, produced the opera-style films *The Fisherman's Revenge*, *Mei Long Town* (with Ma Lian-liang), *Spring of Jade Hall* (with Yu Zhen-fei). However, they were trapped there because of wars.

张君秋（1947）
Zhang Jun-qiu(1947).

① 在香港与马连良、俞振飞合影（1950）
A Photo taken with Ma Lian-liang and Yu Zhen-fei(1950).

② 在戏曲影片《梅龙镇》中饰李凤姐，马连良饰正德皇帝（1949）
In the film opera *Mei Long Town* as Sister Li Feng, Ma Lian-liang as Emperor Zheng De(1949).

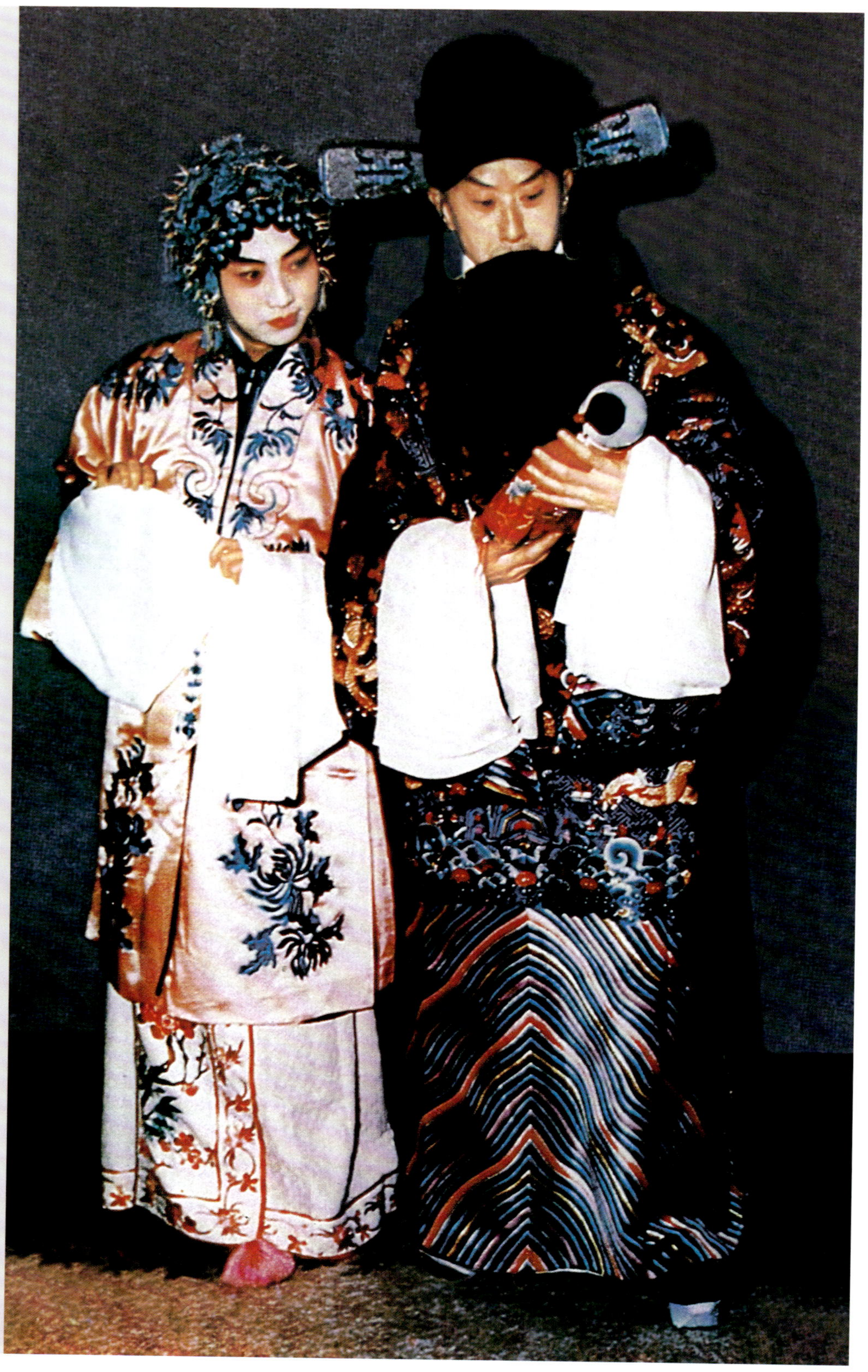

《春秋笔》中饰王妻，马连良饰王彦丞
In *Chun Qiu Bi* as Mrs. Wang, Ma Lian-liang as Wang Yan-cheng.

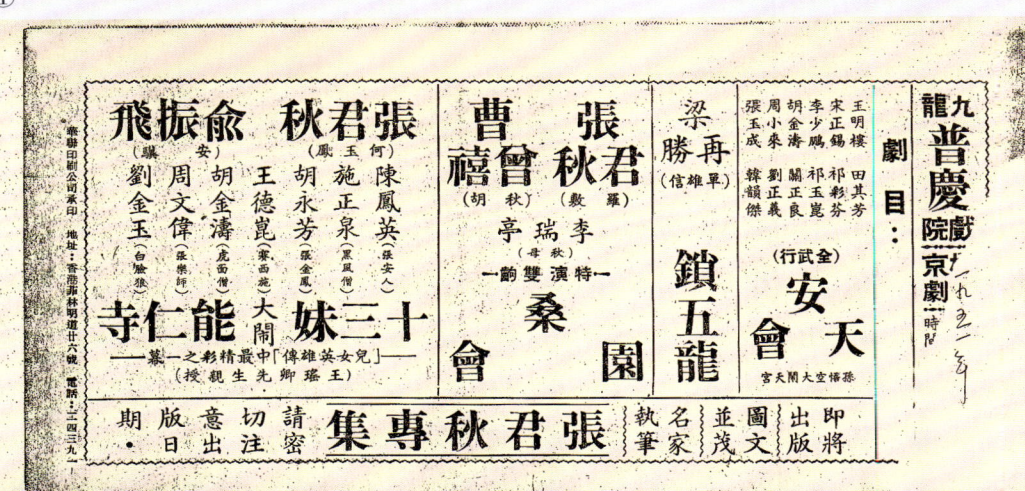

① 在香港同马连良（前排左四）、李慕良（前排右一）等
With Ma Lian-liang (front row, fourth left) Li Mu-liang (front row, first right)in Hong Kong.

② 1951年在香港演出戏报
Performing in Hong Kong in 1951.

③ 1948年香港出版的张君秋等演出专集
Performance albums of Zhang Jun-qiu and others were issued in Hong Kong (1948).

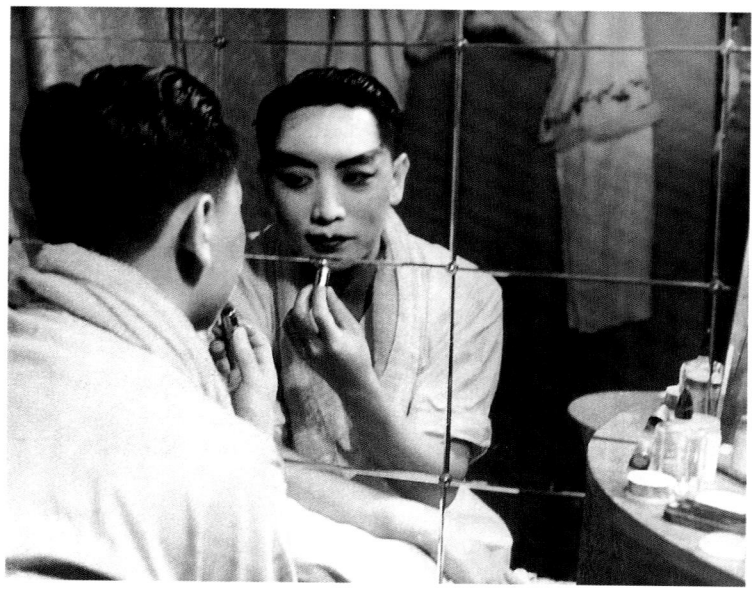

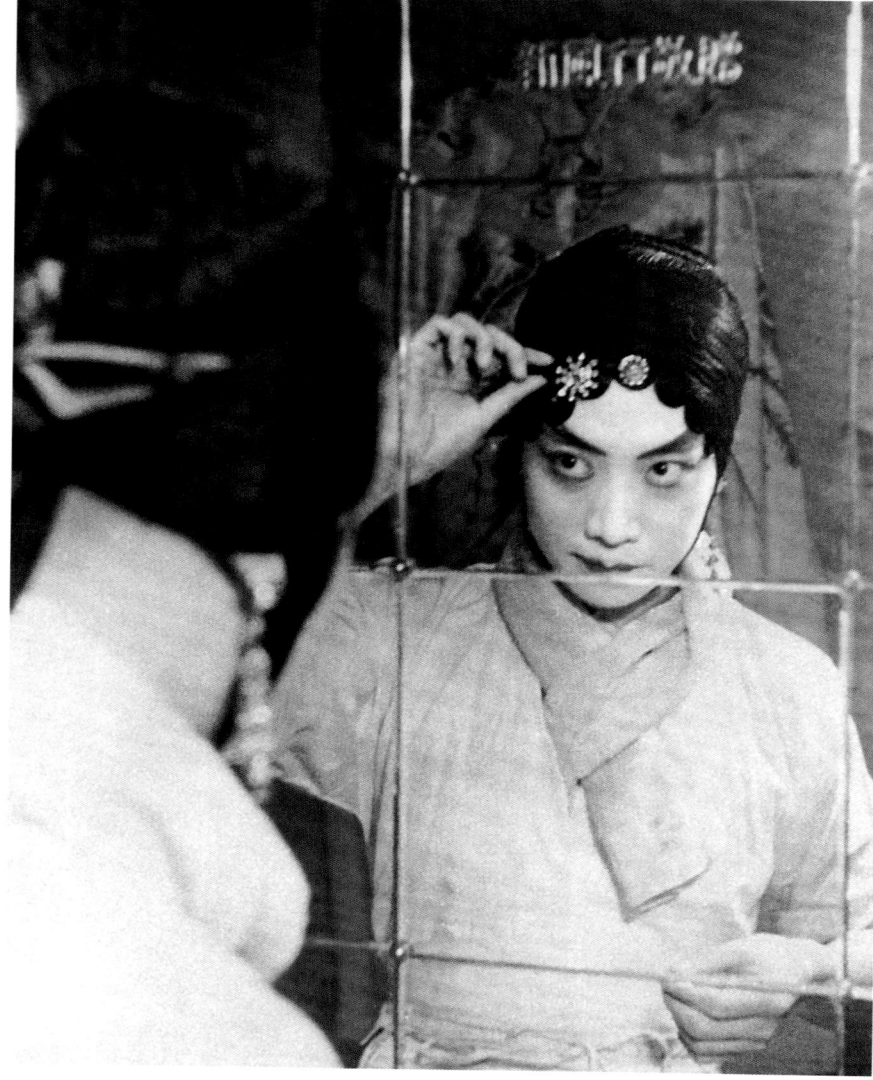
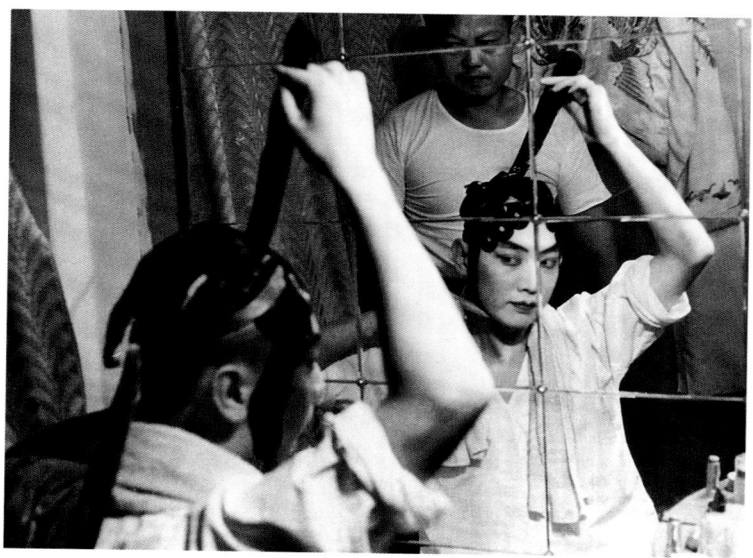

化妆
Putting on make-up.

1951年，张君秋回到内地，受到党政军人士的热烈欢迎。周恩来总理接见了他，鼓励他"为社会主义多做贡献"。张君秋先后加入中南京剧团、北京市京剧三团、北京京剧团。他深入基层演出，参加赴朝慰问团。
他本着"去芜存菁"的原则，整理演出了大量优秀传统剧目，创作演出了《望江亭》、《西厢记》、《状元媒》等大量新编历史剧目，创立了深受观众喜爱的张派艺术。

1951 witnessed Zhang's return to the mainland and his warm welcome by people from the Party, the Political circle and the Army. Premier Zhou En-lai granted an audience to him and encouraged him to "make more contribution to socialism". Zhang was once a member of Central-South Peking Opera Troupe, the Third Branch of Beijing Peking Opera Troupe and Peking Opera Troupe of Beijing. Zhang often went down to the grass roots for performance and participated the visiting performance to North Korea. Based on the principle "discarding the dross and selecting the essential ", Zhang arranged and performed volumes of excellent traditional plays, created and performed a great deal of new historical plays such as *Riverside Pavilion*, the *Western Chamber* and *Top Scholar to Be Matchmaker* and founded the Zhang's art which is extremely popular with the public.

INNOVATION 创新篇

重焕青春 Another Bloom of Youth **推陈出新** Weeding Through the Old to Bring Forth the New
唱腔创新 Innovation of Aria **创立张派** The Foundation of Zhang's School

重焕青春　Another Bloom of Youth

1951年10月28日，张君秋从香港回到内地，在深圳受到党政军人士的热烈欢迎。1952年，周恩来总理接见了他。张君秋激动地对总理说："我回来晚了。"周总理对他说："革命不分先后，爱国不分早晚，回来就好。希望你多做贡献。"张君秋回到内地，最初同马连良一起加入中南京剧团。1952年，张君秋在北京组建北京市京剧三团。1957年，张君秋同马连良、谭富英、裘盛戎等成立了北京京剧团。张君秋在《永远跟着共产党》一文中回忆这段经历时写道："剧团的人事固定，资金稳定，许多在旧戏班难以解决的种种人事问题纷纷迎刃而解，我的全部精力都用在了艺术的改革工作上了。那时候，我们整理、创作演出的剧目一个接着一个，全团的艺术水平得到了普遍的提高，我身上有一股使不完的劲儿，一年下来一统计，三百六十天，平均每天我演一场戏。"1956年张君秋参加祖国亲人慰问志愿军代表团，赴朝慰问志愿军，在冰天雪地里为志愿军战士演出，演完一出《白蛇传》大戏之后，应志愿军战士的要求，毫不犹豫地加演另一出大戏《霸王别姬》。张君秋以极大的热情深入基层演出，并深入到工厂、农村参加劳动，同广大工农群众建立了深厚的友情。

On October 28th, 1951, Zhang returned from Hong Kong and received warm welcome by people from the Party, the Political circle and the Army. In 1952, Premier Chou En-lai granted an audience to him. Zhang passionately told Premier zhou, "I come back late!" But Premier zhou answered, "All patriots belong to one big family, whether they rally to the common cause early or late. The point is you have come back! I hope you will make greater contribution!" After coming back to the mainland, Zhang first joined Central-South Peking Opera Troupe together with Ma Lian-liang. In 1952, Zhang founded the Third Branch of Beijing Peking Opera Troupe. In 1957, Zhang together with Ma Lian-liang, Tan Fu-ying and Qiu Sheng-rong founded Peking Opera Troupe of Beijing. In Always Adhere to the Communist Party, Zhang recalled, "The stability of both personnel and funds helps to smooth away many kinds of personnel problems which were indeterminable in the old troupe. Therefore, I can devote myself wholeheartedly to the innovation of art. At that time, one play that we have created and performed succeeded to another. A general promotion of the artistic proficiency was seen among the whole troupe. I am just filled with inexhaustible drive. For the whole year, I performed, on an average, one play each day." In 1956, Zhang became a member of the-motherland-visiting-volunteer troops-delegation and went to North Korea for a visiting performance. They performed in the dead winter for the volunteer troops and after *The Legend of Lady White Snake*, in order to meet the demand of the volunteers, they had no hesitation in another performance of *Farewell My Concubine*. Zhang went down to the grass roots for performance with immense enthusiasm and shared in physical labor with workers and farmers and thus established deep friendship with them.

张君秋（1951）
Zhang Jun-qiu (1951).

① 演出前与何顺信试音、调弦（50年代）
Sound trial and stringed instrument tune before performance with He Shun-xin (1950s).

②《凤还巢》中饰程雪娥
In *Phoenix Back to Its Nest* as Cheng Xue-e.

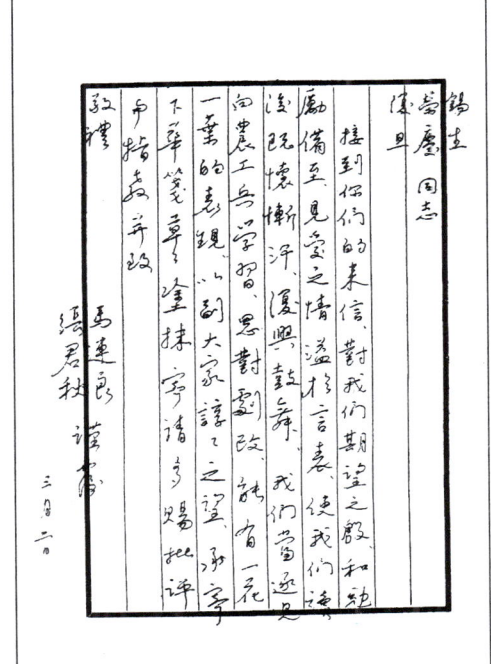

① 马连良、张君秋从香港回内地不久，南京陈锡生等三位大学生给他们写信，并求题词。张、马二位很快复信并题词，表达了他们当时的心情

Soon after Ma Lian-liang and Zhang Jun-qiu's back to the mainland from Hong Kong, three college students wrote to them and asked for inscription. They two replied soon, expressing their feelings at that time.

② 与马连良合影（1951年）

A photo taken with Ma Lian-liang (1951).

① 同荀慧生在一起（1952）
Together with Xun Hui-sheng (1952).

② 同刘雪涛（1954）
Together with Liu Xue-tao (1954).

③ 在南京与何顺信（前排右一，琴师）、金瑞林（前排左二，鼓师）、张似云（前排左一，二胡伴奏）等北京市京剧三团乐队人员合影
A photo taken in Nanjing with the band members of Beijing Peking Opera Troupe 3:He Shun-xin (front row, first right, Music Master), Jin Rui-lin (front row, second left, Drummer), Zhang Si-yun (front row, first left, Erhu Player).

①

②

① 在朝鲜参加慰问志愿军演出时留影。陈少霖（左一）、高乐青（左四）、郑慧荣（左六）、张君秋（右三）（1956）
A photo taken in the visiting performance for the volunteer troop in North Korea. 1st left: Chen Shao-lin, 4th left: Gao Le-qing, 6th left: Zheng Hui-rong, 3rd right: Zhang Jun-qiu (1956).

② 赴朝慰问归来后在颐和园合影（1956）
A photo taken in the Summer Palace after the visiting performance in North Korea (1956).

推陈出新

Weeding Through the Old to Bring Forth the New

在北京市京剧三团时期，张君秋在党的文艺方针指导下，开始了艺术创新之路。本着"去芜存菁"的原则，张君秋整理演出了大量的传统剧目，如《春秋配》、《金山寺、断桥、雷峰塔》、《大保国、探皇灵、二进宫》、《银屏公主》、《红鬃烈马》、《四郎探母》、《玉堂春》、《法门寺》等，修改恢复演出了他在"谦和社"时期创演的新剧目《怜香伴》，创演了《彩楼记》、《刘兰芝》、《望江亭》等新剧目。1956年12月，张君秋领导的北京市京剧三团同马连良领导的马连良京剧团和谭富英、裘盛戎领导的北京市京剧二团合并为北京京剧团（现北京京剧院），陆续创演了《珍妃》、《秋瑾》、《秦香莲》（与马连良、谭富英、裘盛戎合作）、《赵氏孤儿》（与马连良、谭富英、裘盛戎合作）、《西厢记》（与叶盛兰、杜近芳合作）、《状元媒》（与马连良、谭富英合作）、《楚宫恨》（与谭富英合作）、《诗文会》、《年年有余》以及《芦荡火种》等。

When in the Third Branch of Beijing Peking Opera Troupe, Zhang, under the guidance of the Party's artistic policy, went about the innovation of art. Based on the principle "discarding the dross and selecting the essential", Zhang arranged and performed volumes of excellent traditional plays, such as The *Match of Spring and Autumn*, *Jin Shan Buddhist Temple*, *Broken Bridge* and *Lei Feng Pagoda*, *Da Bao Empire* and *Entering the Palace for the Second Time*, *Princess Yin Ping*, *High-Spirited Horses with Red Long Hair*, *Si Lang Visits His Mother*, *Spring in Jade Hall*, *Fa Men Temple*; he also perfected and performed the new play *A Gentle Companion* created when he was in Qian He Troupe; he created and performed some new plays, such as the *Legend of the Color Building*, *Liu Lan Zhi* and *Riverside Pavilion*. In December 1956, Zhang's the Third Branch of Beijing Peking Opera Troupe, Ma Lian-liang's Peking Opera troupe and Qiu Sheng-rong's the Second Branch of Peking Opera of Beijing were consolidated into Peking Opera Troupe of Beijing (Peking Opera Theater of Beijing). They created and performed in succession *Concubine Zhen*, *Qiu Jin*, *Qin Xiang Lian* (together with Ma Lian-liang, Tan Fu-ying and Qiu Sheng-rong), The *Orphan of Zhao Family* (together with Ma Lian-liang, Tan Fu-ying and Qiu Sheng-rong), The *West Chamber* (together with Ye Sheng-lan and Du Jin-fang), *Match Made by scholar Number One* (together with Ma Lian-liang and Tan Fu-ying), *The Story in the Palace of Chu* (together with Tan Fu-ying), *A Meeting of Poets*, *Prosperity*, and *Sparks of Reed Marshes*.

张君秋（1953）
Zhang Jun-qiu(1953).

前排左起：荀慧生、梅兰芳、姜妙香、尚小云；
后排左起：费文芝、梅葆玖、张君秋（1952）
Front row from left: Xun Hui-sheng, Mei Lan-fang, Jiang Miao-xiang, Shang Xiao-yun; back row from left: Fei Wen-zhi, Mei Bao-jiu, Zhang Jun-qiu (1952).

《三娘教子》中饰王春娥,马连良饰薛保(1952)
In *The Third Mistress Brings Up the Son* as Wang Chun-e; Ma Lian-liang as Xue Bao (1952).

① 《回荆州》中饰孙尚香（1952）
In *Liu Bei Returns to Jing Zhou* as Sun Shangxiang (1952).

② 张君秋演出《回荆州》时用的帔
Cape used when performing *Liu Bei Returns to Jing Zhou*.

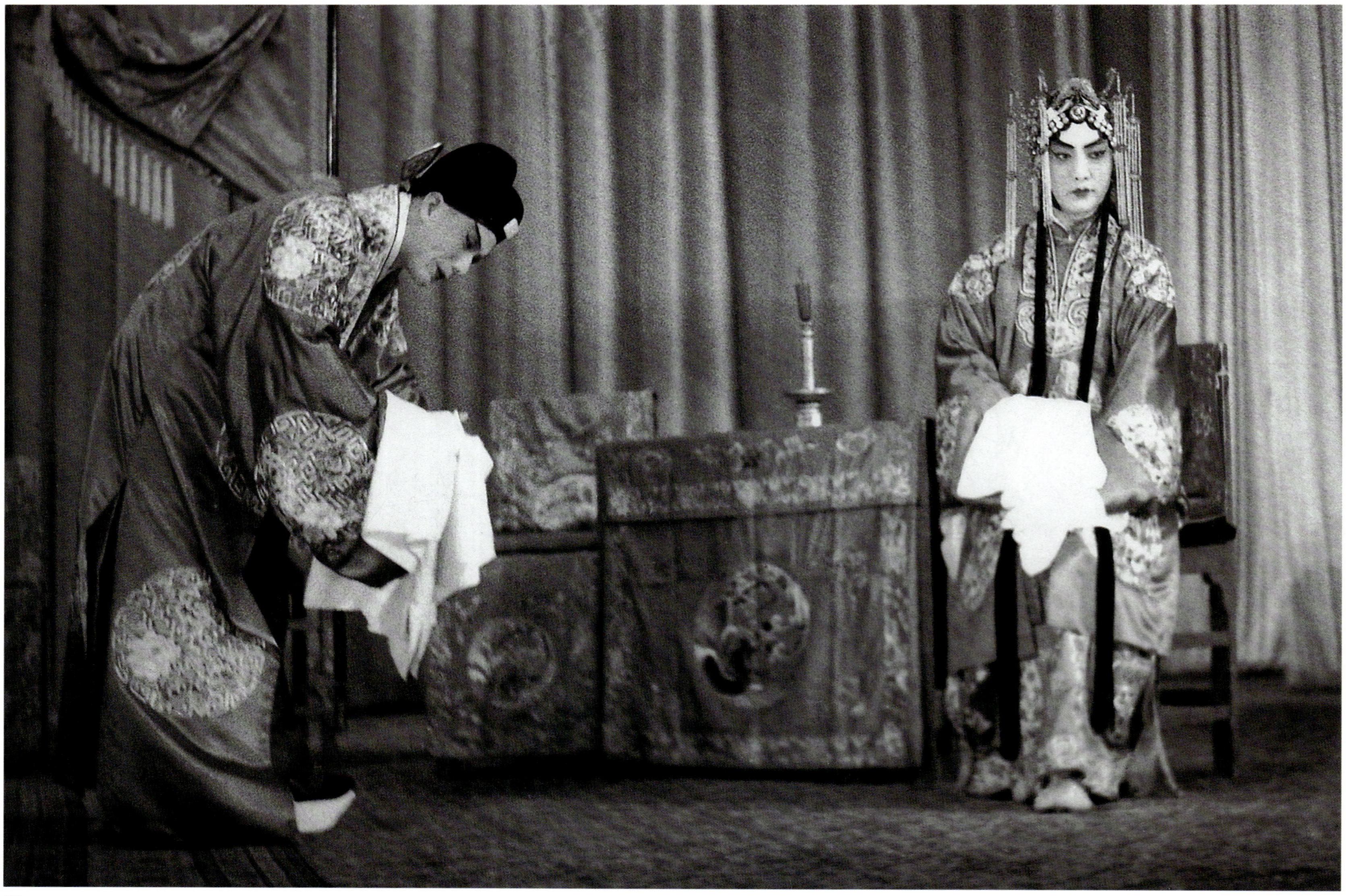

创新篇
推陈出新

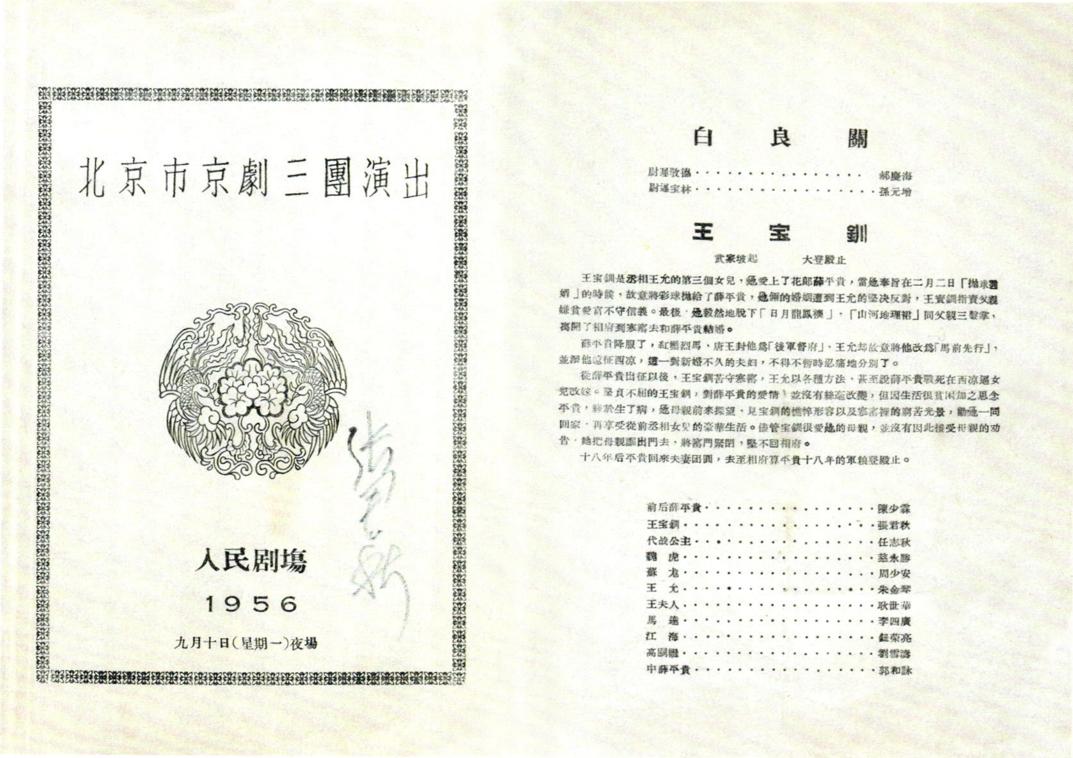

①《凤还巢》中饰程雪娥，刘雪涛饰穆居易（1953）
In *Phoenix Back to Its Nest* as Cheng Xue-e; Liu Xue-tao as Mu Ju-yi (1953).

② 1956年9月10日北京市京剧三团在人民剧场演出《王宝钏》戏单，内有张君秋亲笔签名
The performing list of *Wang Bao Chuan*, which has Zhang Jun-qiu's signature, played by the performers of the third branch of Beijing Peking Opera Troupe on September 10th 1956.

①《女起解》中饰苏三,李四广饰崇公道(1954)
In *Miss Su San Goes to Trial* as Su San; Li Si-guang as Chong Gong-dao (1954).

②《怜香伴》中饰崔笺云(1953)
In *A Gentle Companion* as Cui Jian-yun (1953).

①在《武家坡》中饰王宝钏
In *Wu Jia Po* as Wang Bao-chuan.

②在《大登殿》中饰王宝钏，陈少霖饰薛平贵
In *Great Palace* as Wang Bao-chuan, Chen Shao-lin as Xue Ping-gui.

《南山化蝶》中饰祝英台（50年代）
In *The Eternal Love* as Zhu Ying-tai (1950s).

① 北京市京剧工作者联合会成立时，张君秋同京剧艺术家们座谈讨论。左起：郝寿臣、尚小云、梅兰芳、马连良、李万春、张君秋（1956）
Zhang Jun-qiu discussed with Peking Opera artists at the foundation of Peking Opera Association of Beijing. From left: Hao Shou-chen, Shang Xiao-yun, Mei Lan-fang, Ma Lian-liang, Li Wan-chun, Zhang Jun-qiu (1956).

② 北京市京剧工作者联合会成立大会后代表们合影。左起：马连良、李万春、张梦庚、刘雪涛、梅兰芳、姜妙香、曾平、高乐春、裘盛戎、张仲杰、洪维才、郝友、奚啸伯、陈少霖、许姬传、沈玉斌、王静波、张君秋（1956）
Group photo of the delegation after the founding of Peking Opera Association of Beijing. From the left: Ma Lian-liang, Li Wan-chun, Zhang Meng-geng, Liu Xue-tao, Mei Lan-fang, Jiang Miao-xiang, Zeng Ping, Gao Le-chun, Qiu Sheng-rong, Zhang Zhong-jie, Hong Wei-cai, Hao You, Xi Xiao-bo, Chen Shao-lin, Xu Ji-chuan, Shen Yu-bin, Wang Jing-bo, Zhang Jun-qiu (1956).

① 《四郎探母》中饰铁镜公主，萧长华、马富禄饰国舅（1956）
In *Si Lang Visits His Mother* as Princess Tie Jing; Xiao Chang-hua, Ma Fu-lu as brothers of the empress dowager (1956).

② 《梅龙镇》中饰李凤姐，马连良饰正德皇帝（50年代）
In *Mei Long Town* as Sister Li Feng; Ma Lian-liang as Emperor Zheng De (1950s).

①

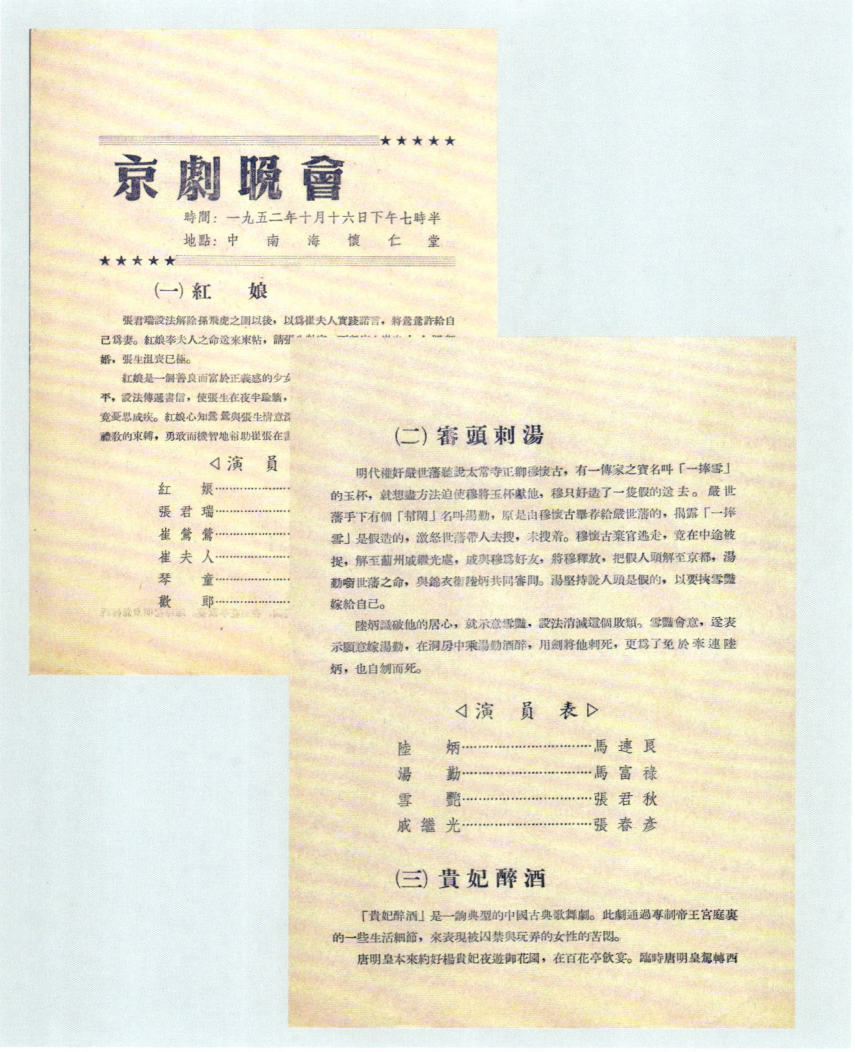

②

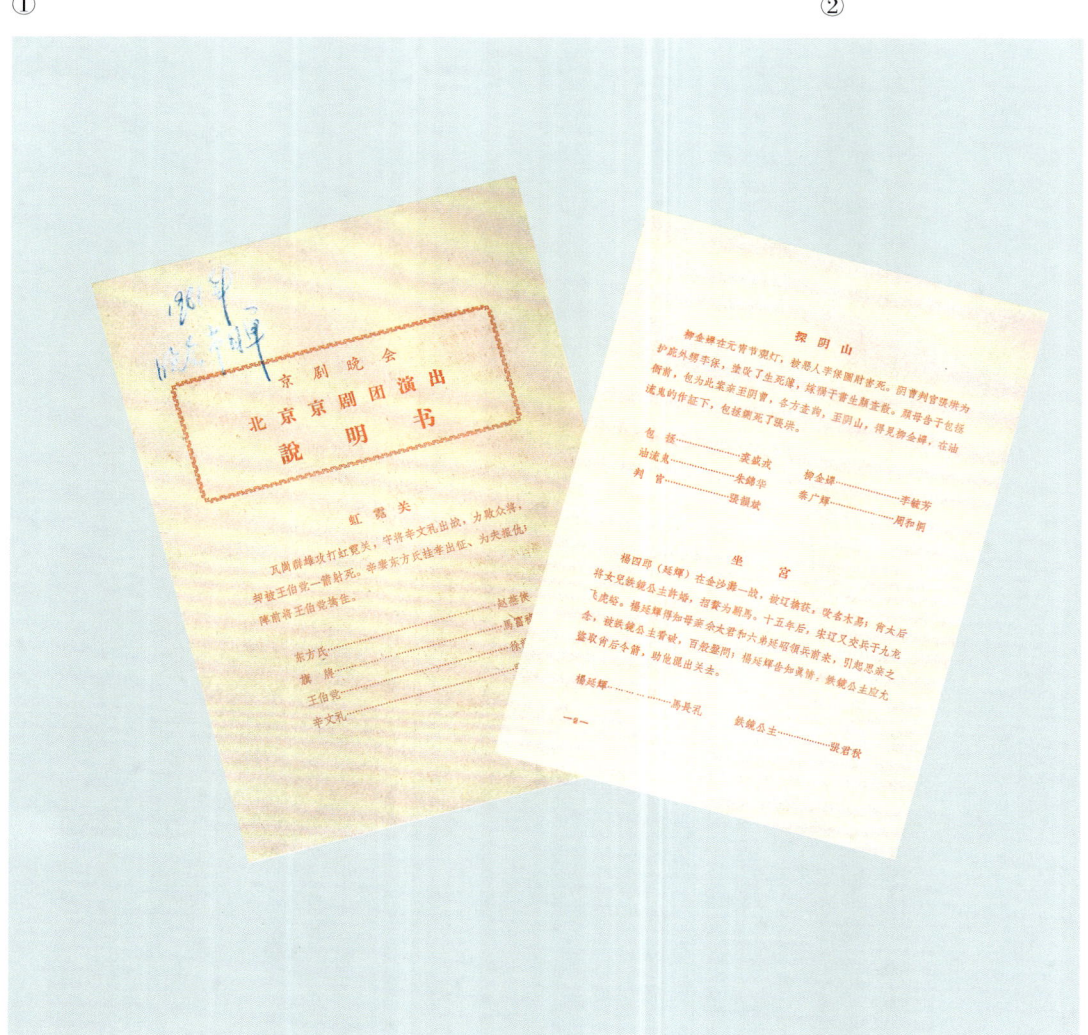

③

① 《四郎探母》中饰铁镜公主（1956）
In Si Lang Visits His Mother as Princess Tie Jing (1956).

② 周恩来、邓颖超保存的张君秋同马连良率中南京剧团到北京演出的节目单
The performing list, saved by Zhou En-lai and Deng Ying-chao, of Zhang Jun-qiu and Ma Lian-liang leading the Central South Peking Opera Troupe to play in Beijing.

③ 周恩来、邓颖超保存的节目单，节目单上的书写文字为邓颖超的笔迹
The scriptures on the performing list, saved by Zhou En-lai and Deng Ying-chao, were written by Deng Ying-chao.

①彭真观看马连良、张君秋演出的《青霞丹雪》后与演员合影
After seeing *Green Rosy Clouds and Red Snow* led by Ma Lian-liang and Zhang Jun-qiu, Peng Zhen took photo with the performers.

②梅兰芳、福芝芳夫妇，张君秋、吴励箴夫妇，与许姬传、谢虹雯、梅葆玥等（1961）
The couple of Mei Lan-fang and Fu Zhi-fang, The couple of Zhang Jun-qiu and Wu Li-zhen had a photo taken with Xu Ji-chuan, Xie Hong-wen and Mei Bao-yue (1961).

与马连良（前右一）、谭富英（前右二）、裘盛戎（后左一）在一起（1957）
Together with Ma Lian-liang (front row, 1st right), Tan Fu-ying (front row, 2nd right), Qiu Sheng-rong (back row, 1st left) (1957).

唱腔创新 Innovation of Aria

青年时代张君秋的创新意识多受王瑶卿和程砚秋的影响。程砚秋创作《锁麟囊》一剧时，常向王瑶卿请教，张君秋多在旁聆听。在《锁麟囊》千变万化的行腔中，张君秋逐渐意识到，人物情感的变化可以使京剧的各种声腔、板式发生各种不同的组合变化，而演唱技巧的自如运用又能赋予声腔艺术千姿百态的新生命。于是，张君秋的心里逐渐萌生了创新的意识。他尝试着在《大登殿》的[二六板]"花郎汉"三字的行腔上做了些变化，演出中用了这个新腔，很受观众欢迎，并得到王瑶卿的首肯。程砚秋告诉他说："咱们的脑子就好比是仓库，存了不少零件（指音乐因素），不定什么时候，把这些零件攒攒，又是一个新机器（指新腔）。"张君秋牢记这些教导，多听多记，并努力用心锤炼自己的演唱技巧。这以后，他在《怜香伴》、《刘兰芝》、《彩楼记》等剧中的唱腔上逐渐放开了手脚进行创新，又在《大保国、二进宫》、《雷峰塔》、《玉堂春》、《红鬃烈马》、《四郎探母》等传统戏的行腔中对原有的声腔板式做了更大幅度的创新。直到《望江亭》，他的唱腔创新能力已经到了炉火纯青的地步。人们开始意识到，一个新的流派艺术就要诞生了。

Zhang's innovative ideas in his youth were greatly influenced by Wang Yao-qing and Cheng Yan-qiu. When Cheng Yan-qiu created *The Jewelry Pouch*, he always asked Wang Yao-qing for advice and Zhang often listened respectfully. In the various arias of *The Jewelry Pouch*, Zhang gradually realized that characters' emotional changes might bring about the combination changes of arias and times. The free operation of vocal acrobatics may endow the art of aria with life. Therefore, Zhang hit upon the idea of innovation. He tried to make variation on the vocal acrobatics of two and six plate "Hua Lang Han" in *Great Palace*. He adopted this new aria in the performance. It was extremely popular with the public and got the approval of Wang Yao-qing. Cheng Yan-qiu told him, "Our brain is like a storage which has a lot of attachments (referred to as musical factors here). You won't know when you will put them together and then a new machine (referred to as aria here) appears." Zhang kept all these in mind, seeing more and noting more, and tried hard to practice his aria. From then on, he gradually went about innovation of aria in *A Gentle Companion*, *Liu Lan Zhi* and The *Legend of the Color Building*. He continued to make even greater changes on the arias and times of some excellent traditional plays, such as *Da Bao Empire and Entering the Palace for the Second Time*, *Lei Feng Pagoda*, *Spring in Jade Hall*, *High-Spirited Horses with Red Long Hair* and *Si Lang Visits His Mother*. Until *Riverside Pavilion*, his aria had already reached a high degree of excellence. People began to realize that a new school of art was coming into being.

张君秋（1955）
Zhang Jun-qiu (1955).

1989年，张君秋荣获金唱片奖
Zhang Jun-qiu was awarded "Golden Phonograph Record Prize" in 1989.

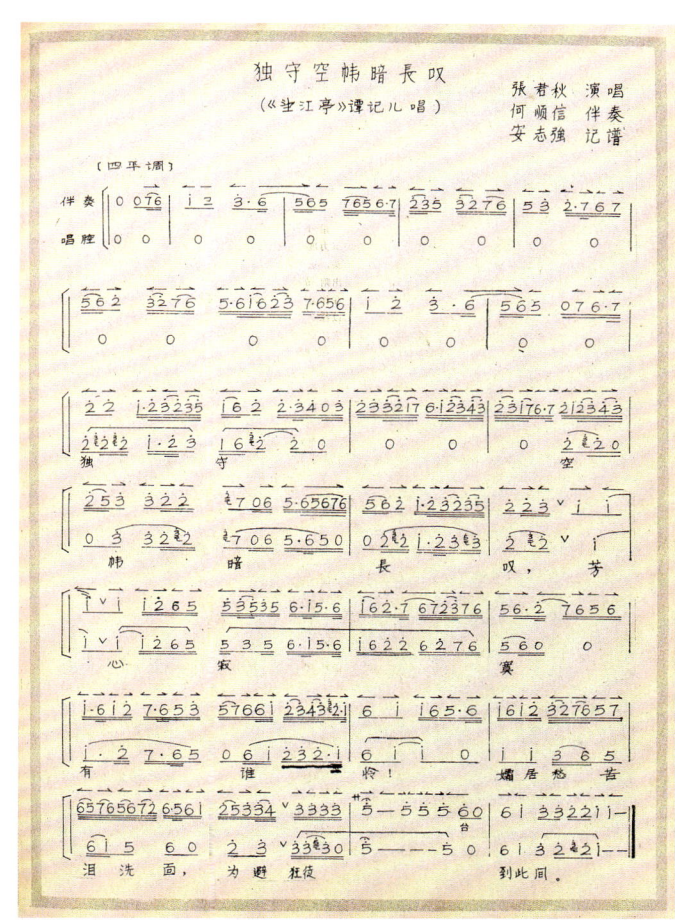

① 《望江亭》中饰谭记儿
In *Riverside Pavilion* as Tan Ji-er.

② 《望江亭》曲谱
Collection of music scores of *Riverside Pavilion*.

③ 1984年何顺信在《中国戏剧》杂志发表的谈《望江亭》伴奏文章影印
The photographic printing of *On Accompanies of Riverside Pavilion* published in *Chinese Theatre* by He Shun-xin, 1984.

④ 张君秋唱腔集（CD）
The Aria Collection of Zhang Jun-qiu (CD).

唱腔创新

① 《西厢记》中饰崔莺莺，刘雪涛饰张珙，耿世华饰崔夫人，赵乃华饰红娘（1979）
In *The West Chamber* as Cui Ying-ying; Liu Xue-tao as Zhang Sheng, Geng Shi-hua as Madam Cui, Zhao Nai-hua as Hong Niang(1979).

② 张君秋1980年在《戏剧报》发表的有关《西厢记·赖婚》一场唱腔的文章影印
The photographic printing of *On the Aria of The West Chamber* published in *Drama Newspaper* by Zhang Jun-qiu in 1980.

创立张派
The Foundation of Zhang School

张君秋艺术创作最旺盛的时期是在50年代中期至60年代中期。这期间，他致力于剧本、音乐、表演、化妆、服饰等多方面的革新。他演出经过整理加工的《起解、会审》《金山寺、断桥、雷峰塔》、《祭江》、《银屏公主》、《春秋配》、《三娘教子》、《法门寺》、《大保国、探皇灵、二进宫》、《四郎探母》、《红鬃烈马》、《刘兰芝》等传统剧目，思想性、艺术性均有提高。他主演的《彩楼记》、《珍妃》、《望江亭》、《西厢记》、《诗文会》、《楚宫恨》、《秦香莲》、《状元媒》、《秋瑾》、《赵氏孤儿》、《年年有余》等，更以艺术的精湛而深受广大观众及戏曲界同行的赞誉。他善于在京剧旦角传统唱腔的基础上，吸收其他行当及兄弟剧种、曲艺、歌曲的音乐元素，创作出大量的新腔。他的演唱，充分发挥了嗓音"娇、媚、脆、水"的优异天赋，同时悉心揣摩梅兰芳、程砚秋、荀慧生、尚小云等各派旦角演唱艺术的风采而加以融会贯通。他的发音，强调全身的松弛，保持共鸣位置的准确和行腔运气的畅通，因而音域十分宽广。行腔讲究轻重、快慢、繁简的对比，并善于在胡琴伴奏音乐的配合下，巧妙地蓄气、缓气、偷气，因而他的演唱音色绚丽，感情丰富，舒展自如，形成了华丽柔美、刚健清新的独特风格。表演身段端庄含蓄，自然率真。在化妆服饰等方面，讲究色调同人物身份、性格的美观协调。张君秋的艺术创造，使中国京剧的艺术画廊中增添了谭记儿、崔莺莺、秦香莲等聪明秀丽、勇于同旧势力抗争的中国古代妇女形象。张派艺术是中华人民共和国建国以来京剧事业繁荣昌盛的重要标志。

张君秋还参加过《海棠峪》、《红色娘子军》、《平原作战》等剧目的唱腔音乐设计工作。他主演的《望江亭》、《秦香莲》先后摄制成戏曲舞台艺术影片。

Mid 1950s to mid 1960s is the most productive period of time in Zhang's artistic creation. During that period of time, he devoted himself to the innovation of drama, music, performance, face making and costume. He performed those revised excellent traditional plays like *Convey*, *Joint Hearing*, *Jin Shang Buddhist Temple*, *Broken Bridge* and *Lei Feng Pagoda*, *Sacrifice at the Riverside*, *Princess Yin Pin*, *The Match of Spring and Autumn*, *The Third Mistress Brings up the Son*, *Fa Men Temple*, *Da Bao Empire* and *Entering the Palace for the Second Time*, *Si Lang Visits His Mother*, *High-Spirited Horses with Red Long Hair* and *Liu Lan Zhi* with an improved artistry and thoughtfulness. *The Legend of Color Building*, *Concubine Zhen*, *Riverside Pavilion*, *The West Chamber*, *A Meeting of Poets*, *The Story in the Palace of Chu*, *Qin Xiang Lian*, *Top Scholar to Be a Matchmaker*, *Qiu Jin*, *The Orphan of Zhao Family*, *Prosperity* featuring him as the lead, won him the acclaim of both the public and the experts in the walks of drama with their artistic excellence. On the basis of the traditional aria of the female role, he was good at assimilating elements of other roles, dramas, and songs to create volumes of new arias. His gifted voice is characterized by "soft, charming, crisp and juicy". In the meantime, he carefully fathomed out and made it a part of his own the singing manners of female roles of different schools like Mei Lan-fang, Cheng Yan-qiu, Xun Hui-sheng and Shang Xiao-yun. His manner of singing gave prominence to total physical relax, keeping an exact resonance position and the smooth of cavity and air current, and therefore had an extremely wide range. The operation of cavity emphasized the contrast among lightness and heaviness, quickness and slowness, complexity and simplicity. He was also good at, with the combination of Chinese violin, storing air, having a respite and stealing air so that his voices presented beautifully with an abundant emotion which was bright and gorgeous and full of feelings in his fluent singing. His figures on stage were solemn and sincere in nature. In face making and costume, he was fastidious about the coordination between the color of the clothes and the disposition of the characters. Zhang's artistic innovation added to the Chinese traditional gallery a series of bright and brave ancient Chinese women like Tan Ji-er, Cui Ying-ying and Qin Xiang-lian. (Zhang's) school marked the prosperity of Peking Opera since the founding of People's Republic of China.

Zhang also participated in the aria design of the plays as *The Valley of Cherry-apple*, *The Red Detachment of Women* and *Battle on the Plain Riverside Pavilion* and *Qin Xiang Lian* in which he was a leading role were made into drama art films.

《望江亭》中饰谭记儿

In *Riverside Pavilion* as Tan Ji-er.

【金山寺、断桥、祭塔】 Jin Shan Buddhist Temple, Broken Bridge, Sacrifice to the Tower

白蛇因羡慕人间生活,来到尘世,化名白素贞同许仙结为美满姻缘。法海蓄意破坏他们的婚姻,在端阳节时使白素贞误饮雄黄酒,现出蛇身,许仙受惊,入金山寺参禅。白素贞携小青到金山寺恳求法海放出许仙,法海不允,白素贞水淹金山,许仙逃下山来,夫妻和好如初,生下一子。法海率神将追踪而至,以金钵拘白素贞,压在雷峰塔下。许仙之子许士林长大成人,得中状元,赴雷峰塔祭拜其母,白素贞被塔神允见,向许士林尽诉前情。

这是张君秋在"谦和社"时期走红的剧目,日后不断加工修改,成为张君秋的长期保留剧目。张君秋饰演白素贞。"金山寺"唱的是昆腔,载歌载舞,翻打扑跌;"断桥"唱的是[西皮],"雷峰塔"(又名《祭塔》,以单折演出)以成套[反二黄]唱腔压底,荡气回肠。是一出允文允武,昆乱不挡的重头戏。由此可以看出张君秋唱、念、做、舞艺术功力全面深厚。

Being envious of human beings' life, the White Snake came to the world and she used an alias as Bai Su-zhen and married Xu Xian, living a happy life. Fa Hai, a monk intentionally broke up their marriage. In the Dragon Boat Festival, he lured Bai Su-zhen into drinking the realgar wine which broke open her nature as a snake. Xu Xian was extremely frightened and went to Jin Shan Buddhist Temple for meditation. Bai Su-zhen, together with the Green Snake, pleaded Fa Hai to release Xu Xian in failure. Therefore, Bai flushed out Jin Shan Buddhist Temple and Xu Xian escaped from the mountain. The couple came to terms with each other and gave birth to a child. Fa Hai with many officers and soldiers used the golden earthen bowl to seize Bai Su-zhen who was pressed under the Lei Feng Tower. Xu Shi-lin, Xu Xian's son became the top scholar in the imperial civil service exam and went to Lei Feng Tower to pay a visit to his mother. Bai was admitted by the guard to see her son and told him everything that happened in the past.

This is the popular play when Zhang Jun-qiu was in Qian He Troupe. This play became Zhang's repertoire after continuous revision. Zhang was as Bai Su-zhen. *Jin Shan Buddhist Temple* is of Jiang Su Aria. Singing and dancing, jumping and hitting prevailed the whole play. *Broken Bridge* was of Xi Pi Aria. *Lei Feng Tower* (or *Sacrificing the Tower*, performed by single-fold) pressed the bottom with the aria of anti-Er Huang. It was an important play, requiring both civil and military abilities. From this play, we may see that Zhang had an all-around development in singing, reading, performing and acrobatic fighting.

《金山寺》中饰白素贞
In *Jin Shan Buddhist Temple* as Bai Su-zhen.

① ②《金山寺》中饰白素贞
In *Jin Shan Buddhist Temple* as Bai Su-zhen.

③《祭塔》中饰白素贞（1943）
In *A Sacrifice to the Tower* as Bai Su-zhen (1943).

【玉堂春】 Spring in Jade Hall

　　妓女苏三结识尚书之子王金龙，互相倾慕，约定白头偕老。王金龙千金散尽，被鸨儿赶出院门，又将苏三卖与富商沈燕林为妾。沈妻皮氏同赵监生有奸情，定计在肉面中下毒，欲毒死苏三，却把沈燕林毒死。皮氏买通官府，反诬苏三谋害亲夫，将她屈打成招。王金龙中高科，被任命巡按，闻苏三蒙冤，遂调来苏三亲自审理，使苏三冤情大白。王金龙、苏三破镜重圆。

　　这是张君秋在"谦和社"时期最为叫座的剧目，张君秋饰演苏三。张演此剧多演"起解"、"会审"两折。张君秋在内中各种板式的[西皮]行腔中，充分发挥了他"娇、媚、脆、水"的天赋歌喉，使之声情并茂，脍炙人口。

　　A prostitute named Su San falls in love with a scholar who frequents her brothel. When the scholar runs out of money the procuress bars him from returning. Meanwhile, the prostitute is sold to a merchant from Shanxi Province. The merchant's wife poisons her husband and the prostitute is blamed. The scholar has become a high official in charge of justice at Taiyuan, capital of Shanxi Province. He has questions about the merchant's murder and orders the prostitute to be brought to Taiyuan. He finds the accused is his former lover and is so shocked that he loses his self-composure, which betrays his involvement with her. He pays a private visit to her in jail but is discovered by another official, who is persuaded to investigate the case and find the truth. In the end she is cleared of the charge and is married to her former lover.

　　This is the most popular play when Zhang was in Qian He Troupe. Zhang acted as Su San. Zhang most often played the highlights of "Convey" and "Joint Hearing". Zhang adopted various modes of "Xipi" tune, which exploited his talented voice which was "soft, charming, crisp and juicy". He belted out the play so well that it helped win universal praise.

《玉堂春·苏三起解》中饰苏三（1981）
In *Spring in Jade Hall—The Convey of Su San* as Su San (1981).

《玉堂春·三堂会审》中饰苏三,姜妙香饰王金龙(1963)
In *Spring in Jade Hall—Joint Hearing* as Su San; Jiang Miao-xiang as Wang Jing-long (1963).

【龙凤呈祥】 PROSPERITY Brought by the Dragon and the Phoenix

　　三国，孙权为向刘备讨还荆州，听从周瑜之计，以将其妹孙尚香许配刘备为名，将刘骗哄过江，以为人质。刘备过江，依孔明锦囊妙计，拜访乔国丈，表示诚意。乔国丈以孙、刘和好之事从中周旋，遂使周瑜美人之计弄假成真。刘备、孙尚香喜结良缘。这是张君秋同马连良长期合作演出的传统剧目，张君秋饰演孙尚香。在长期的艺术实践中，张君秋此剧中的演唱日臻完美，"洞房"中的[慢板]唱腔脍炙人口，广为流传。

　　In the period of Three Kingdoms, in order to demand the return of Jing Zhou from Liu Bei, Sun Quan follows the advice of Zhou Yu to deceive Liu to the other bank of the river as the hostage under the disguise of marrying his sister Sun Shang-xiang to Liu Bei. After crossing the river, Liu Bei follows the excellent plan of Kong Ming to visit Qiao Guo Qiao, Father-in-law zhang to show his sincerity. Qiao socializes in the reunion of Sun and Liu, which turns Zhou Yu's Badger Game into a real one. Finally, they happily marry each other.

This is the excellent traditional play co-performed by Zhang Jun-qiu and Ma Lian-liang for a long time. Zhang was as Sun Shang-xiang. In the long term performance, Zhang gradually perfected his manner of singing. The "slow tempo" aria of Nuptial Chamber won universal praise and enjoyed popularity.

①

②

③

① 《龙凤呈祥》中饰孙尚香（80年代）
In *Prosperity Brought by the Dragon and the Phoenix* as Sun Shang-xiang (1980s).

② 《龙凤呈祥》中饰孙尚香，汪正华饰刘备（1982）
In *Prosperity Brought by the Dragon and the Phoenix* as Sun Shang-xiang; Wang Zheng-hua as Liu Bei (1982).

③ 《龙凤呈祥》中饰孙尚香（1982）
In *Prosperity Brought by the Dragon and the Phoenix* as Sun Shang-xiang (1982).

银屏公主
Princess Yin Ping

驸马秦怀玉出征，其子秦英骁勇，因太师詹国丈招摇过市激怒秦英，遂杖击国丈身亡。秦英母银屏公主绑子上殿请罪，长孙皇后从中周旋，太宗念其父征战有功，免秦英死罪，令其领兵戴罪立功。这是张君秋于"谦和社"时期在王瑶卿指点下上演的传统剧目，张君秋饰演银屏公主。内中唱腔有所创新，特别是"金殿"一场中［二六板］唱腔中的"垛句"行腔的唱法颇具新意。是张君秋的长期保留剧目。

The Emperor's son-in-law Qin Huai-yu goes out for a battle. His son Qin Ying who is extremely valiant hits the Grand Tutor Zhan to death due to his swaggering across the street. Qin Ying's mother, princess Yin Ping, ties his son to the court for punishment. Queen Zhang Sun socializes in between. Thinking of his father's fighting for the country, Emperor Tai Zong absolves him and orders him to atone for his crimes by fighting the enemy. This is the traditional play performed by Zhang Jun-qiu when he was in Qian He Troupe under the direction of Wang Yao-qing. Zhang Jun-qiu was as Princess Yin Ping. There is innovation of the aria especially the aria of "Duo Ju" of the "Er Liu Plate" in Palace. This play is Zhang's repertoire.

①

②

【苏武牧羊】 Su Wu as a Sheperd

汉，苏武出使匈奴，匈奴王爱惜苏武，使汉降将卫律劝苏武归顺。苏武坚辞，被押送北海牧羊。十年后，匈奴王以胡阿云赐苏武，苏武推拒，胡阿云敬佩苏武不失气节，遂向苏武表明心迹，苏武始与成婚。后汉帝得知苏武尚在，讨还苏武。匈奴王允苏武回国，但不许胡阿云同行。苏武与胡阿云洒泪分别。

这是张君秋同马连良长期合作演出的剧目。张君秋饰胡阿云。胡阿云的念白是京白，张君秋继承了王瑶卿的"风搅雪"的京白特点，明亮脆爽，清新流畅，刻画了胡阿云这一北国女子的爽朗性格。[西皮慢板]的演唱，细腻地刻画了对苏武的敬佩之情。

In Han dynasty, Su Wu was sent on a diplomatic mission to the Hun. The emperor of Hun liked Su Wu and made the capitulated soldier Wei Lu persuad Su Wu to join Hun. Su directly turned it down and then was sent under escort to tend flocks in Bei Hai. A decade later, the emperor of Hun wanted to marry Hu A'yun to Su Wu and was turned down once more. Hu admired Su's integrity and showed love to him. They two got married. Emperor Wu Ti got the information that Su Wu was still alive and sent troops to ask for Su Wu's return. The emperor of Hun didn't allow Hu A'yun's company with Su Wu. Finally, Su and Hu said farewell to each other in pain.

This is the play joinly performed by Zhang Jun-qiu and Ma Lian-liang for a long time. Zhang was as Hu A'yun. Zhang's spoken part is that of Beijing. Zhang adopted Wang Yao-qing's characteristics of "snowdrift", bright and clear, melodious and fluent, which depicts the bright and comfortable characteristics of Hu, a northern Chinese girl. The singing of "Xipi slow tempo" depicts her admiration of Su Wu in detail.

① 《银屏公主》中饰银屏公主（1981）
In *Princess Yin Ping* as Princess Yin Ping (1981).

② 《银屏公主》中饰银屏公主，李世霖饰李世民
In *Princess Yin Ping* as Princess Yin Ping; Li Shi-lin as Li Shi-min.

③ 《苏武牧羊》中饰胡阿云，马连良饰苏武（60年代）
In *Su Wu as a Sheperd* as Hu A'yun; Ma Lian-liang as Su Wu (1960s).

【春秋配】 The Match of Spring and Autumn

姜秋莲之父出外经商,姜受继母贾氏逼迫,随乳娘到荒郊砍柴。秀才李春发路过荒郊,见姜秋莲病容满面,上前问明原委,赠银一锭,嘱姜买柴回家。姜秋莲感激不尽,请乳娘代为致谢,见李春发谈吐有礼,心无邪念,遂生爱慕之心。这是张君秋在"谦和社"时期上演的剧目,张君秋饰演姜秋莲。建国后,张君秋对此剧做了全面的加工整理,尤其在唱腔上,此中[二黄慢板]及[南梆子]的行腔尤为精到。

Jiang Qiu-lian (Autumn)'s father goes out for business. Forced by her stepmother, Jiang followed her wet nurse to chop wood. Skilful writer Li Chun-fa (Spring) passes by the wildness and sees Autumn's face covered with sickness. He makes clear what has happened to her and gives her some money for medicine. Autumn appreciates it and thanks him a lot. She feels that Spring is gentle and honest and falls in love with him.

This is the play performed when Zhang was in Qian He Troupe. After the foundation of China, Zhang made corrections to perfect it, especially on the aria. The tune using of "Er Huang slow tempo" and "Na Bang Zi Operas" are extremely innovative.

①

②

③

①《春秋配》中饰姜秋莲(80年代)
In *The Match of the Spring and the Autumn* as Jiang Qiu-lian (1980s).

②《春秋配》中饰姜秋莲(1983)
In *The Match of the Spring and the Autumn* as Jiang Qiu-lian (1983).

③《春秋配》中饰姜秋莲(1983)
In *The Match of the Spring and the Autumn* as Jiang Qiu-lian (1983).

①

②

①《春秋配》中饰姜秋莲，俞振飞饰李春发（1981）
In *The Match of the Spring and the Autumn* as Jiang Qiu-lian (1981).

②《春秋配》中饰姜秋莲，刘雪涛饰李春发，耿世华饰乳娘（1983）
In *The Match of the Spring and the Autumn* as Jiang Qiu-lian; Liu Xue-tao as Li Chun-fa; Geng Shi-hua as Wet Nurse (1983).

【怜香伴】 A Gentle Companion

曹有容携女语花入京应试，路经扬州借住雨花庵。秀才崔介夫偶读语花诗，心甚倾慕。语花妹笺云从中说合，曹有容受人挑拨未允。崔介夫因人作梗，又失去功名，懊丧而归。三年后，崔介夫再次应试，曹有容任主考官。笺云献计要崔更名石坚应试。崔依计而行，得以中试。曹有容爱其才，以女语花妻之。及至得知石坚即崔介夫又欲悔婚。笺云定计说服，曹始知受人挑拨，遂允成婚。

这是张君秋在"谦和社"时期创演的第一个新编剧目，张君秋饰演崔笺云。剧中，张君秋在［四平调］、［南梆子］的行腔演唱上做了初步的创新尝试，建国后，又在内容、形式等各方面做了进一步的加工整理。

Cao You-rong carried his daughter Yu Hua to participate in the civil service examination. En route, they lodged in Rain-flower nunnery in Yang Zhou. Skilful writer Cui Jie-fu happened to read a poem written by Yu Hua and showed his great admiration. Jian Yun, Yu Hua's sister brought the two together but the father Cao You-rong who was provoked by others refused it. Cui, who was hindered by others failed in the exam and went back home in disappointment. Three years later, Cui took another exam which was hosted by Cao You-rong. Jian Yu offered Cui the advice of changing his name to Shi Jian (as strong as stone). Cui followed it and succeeded. In favor of his talent, Cao married Yu Hua to him. However Cao wanted to break the promise of marriage when he learnt that Shi Jian was actually Cui Jie-fu. Finally, Jian Yun persuaded Cao into allowing their marriage.

This is the first new play created by Zhang Jun-qiu when he was in Qian He Troupe. Zhang Jun-qiu was as Cui Jian-yun. Zhang made a first innovation on the using of "Si-ping tune" and "Na Bang Zi". After the foundation of China, he continued to perfect it.

①

②

【刘兰芝】 Liu Lan Zhi

庐江小吏焦仲卿娶妻刘兰芝,夫妻相敬如宾。焦母虐待儿媳,百般挑剔,逼迫焦仲卿休妻。兰芝兄刘洪爱财,又将兰芝转嫁他人。焦仲卿闻讯赶来与兰芝相会,二人投江殉情。

这是张君秋建国后根据传统戏《孔雀东南飞》修改整理后演出的剧目,张君秋饰演刘兰芝。"机房"一场的[二黄]唱腔成为脍炙人口的唱段。80年代,由李瑞环撰写唱词,张君秋谱曲,又为"离别"、"投江"等场次中的刘兰芝增添了[南梆子]、[反二黄]等新唱段,使得刘兰芝的唱腔更为丰富。

Beadle Jiao Zhong-qing of Lu Jiang married Liu Lan-zhi and they lived a happy life. Jiao's mother always found faults with her daughter-in-law and forced Jiao to divorce with her. Liu Hong, Liu Lan-zhi's brother was grudging of money and married Liu to someone else. Hearing this news, Jiao came to drown himself in the river together with Liu Lan-zhi for love.

This play was organized and revised according to the traditional play *A Pair of Peacocks Fly Southeast* by Zhang after the foundation of China. Zhang Jun-qiu was as Liu Lan-zhi. The "Er Huang" aria of "Weaving Room" became widely accepted by people. In 1980s, Li Rui-huan wrote the words of the play and Zhang made the melody, which added some new tunes of "Na Bang Zi" and "Anti-Er Huang" to some scenes like "Departure" and "Drowning into the river". This further enriched the arias of Liu Lan-zhi.

③

① ②在《怜香伴》中饰崔笺云(50年代)
In *A Gentle Companion* as Cui Jian-yun(1950s).

③《刘兰芝》中饰刘兰芝,李四广饰焦母,崔鸣仙饰小姑,钮荣亮饰刘洪(1953)
In *Liu Lan Zhi* as Liu Lan-zhi; Li Si-guang as Jiao's mother; Ren Zhi-qiu as younger sister; Niu Rong-liang as Liu Hong (1953).

【彩楼记】 The Legend of Color Building

丞相刘懋之女刘翠屏抛球选婿，被穷秀才吕蒙正得到。刘懋嫌贫爱富，欲悔婚，翠屏不从，随夫吕蒙正至寒窑，靠木兰寺讨斋度日，受尽寺僧百般刁难、讽刺，夫妻贫不改志。刘氏夫人思女成疾，乃暗中相助。及至吕蒙正科场及第返回寒窑，同岳母相聚。

这是张君秋在北京市京剧三团时根据同名川剧移植改编过来的新剧目。

Prime Minister Liu Mao's daughter Liu Cui-ping wants to choose a husband by throwing Embroidered Ball, which is accidentally gotten by a poor scholar named Lu Meng-zheng. Liu Mao dislikes him for poverty and wants to break the promise of marriage. However, Liu Cui-ping falls in love with Lu Meng-zheng and is disobedient to her father. She marries Lu Meng-zheng and lives with him in Mu Lan temple, Ping Yao town where they live as beggars and are severely tortured by the monks. Liu Cui-ping's mother misses her daughter so much that she falls into sickness and helps them secretly. When Lu Meng-zheng passes the imperial examination, she goes to Ping Yao to meet her daughter and son-in-law.

The Legend of Color Building was a new play adapted from the cognominal Sichuan Opera when Zhang Jun-qiu was in the third branch of Beijing Peking Opera Troupe.

①

①《彩楼记》中饰刘翠屏，刘雪涛饰吕蒙正（1954）
In *The Legend of Color Building* as Liu Cui-ping, Liu Xue-tao as Lu Meng-zheng (1954).

②《彩楼记》中饰刘翠屏（1954）
In *The Legend of Color Building* as Liu Cui-ping (1954).

②

① ②《彩楼记》中饰刘翠屏，刘雪涛饰吕蒙正（1954）
In *The Legend of Color Building* as Liu Cui-ping, Liu Xue-tao as Lu Meng-zheng (1954).

③《彩楼记》中饰刘翠屏，刘雪涛饰吕蒙正，耿世华饰刘母，李四广、钮荣亮饰和尚（1954）
In *The Legend of Color Building* as Liu Cui-ping, Liu Xue-tao as Lu Meng-zheng, Geng Hua as Liu Cui-ping's mother, Li Si-guang and Niu Rong-liang as monks (1954).

【 珍妃 】 Concubine Zhen

清，光绪帝在珍妃的帮助下，启用康有为、梁启超变法维新，被袁世凯出卖，变法失败，珍妃被慈禧投掷井内而亡。

这是张君秋在北京京剧团时排演的新剧目，张派唱腔在这出戏里又有了新的发展。

In Qing dynasty, with the help of Concubine Zhen, Emperor appointed Kang You-wei and Liang Qi-chao, who were later betrayed by Yuan Shi-kai, to implement the constitutional reform and modernization. Concubine Zhen was thrown into a well by Empress Dowager after the failure of the constitutional reform.

It was a new play rehearsed in Beijing Peking Opera Theatre, in which Zhang's aria enjoyed new development.

①《珍妃》中饰珍妃（1956）
In *Concubine Zhen* as Concubine Zhen (1956).

②③④⑤演《珍妃》所用过的服装
The costume that he wore in *Concubine Zhen*.

①

②

③

④

⑤

望江亭 Riverside Pavilion

学士李希颜亡故,其妻谭记儿为避太尉之子杨衙内的纠缠,避居清安观,为白道姑抄写经卷。白道姑之侄白士中得中进士,官授潭州太守,赴任途中,路过清安观看望姑母。经白道姑撮合,二人喜结良缘。杨衙内得知,心怀仇恨,乃假造圣旨,私制尚方宝剑,至潭州缉拿白士中。白士中得知,焦虑无措。谭记儿扮成渔妇在望江亭内将杨衙内灌醉,盗取私制的尚方宝剑及圣旨。次日,杨衙内至潭州,方知事情败露。白士中以假冒钦差罪,捕拿杨衙内。

这是张君秋根据川剧《谭记儿》移植改编过来的新剧目,张君秋饰演谭记儿。在这出戏的创作演出中,张君秋的唱腔艺术创作已经到了炉火纯青的境界,内中[四平调]、[二黄摇板转三眼、原板]、[南梆子]以及[二六板]的演唱使人既似曾相识,又耳目一新,很快得到广泛流传。这是张派艺术得以确立的扛鼎之作。

Tan Ji-er, dead scholar Li Xi-yan's wife, sheltered herself in Qing An Temple to escape from being pestered by Prime Minister's on Master Yang and did copying for the taoist nun Bai.Bai Shi-zhong, the nephew of the Taoist nun Bai, was entitled as the successful candidate in the highest imperial examinations, and then he was designated as the head of Tan Zhou. On his way to the official position, he went to see his aunt, who acted as the go-between of his marriage with Tan Ji-er. Knowning this, Master Yang was so jealous that he forged an imperial decree and an emperor's sword in order to arrest Bai Shi-zhong. Hearing of this, Bai Shi-zhong was at a loss. Tan Ji-er disguised herself as a fishwoman and successfully stole the forged imperial decree and the emperor's sword by making Master Yang drunk. It was in the next day when Master Yang arrived at Tan Zhou that he found his conspiracy exposed.Bai Shi-zhong arrested Master Yang in the name of passing himself off as the imperial envoy.

Riverside Pavilion was a new play adapted from the Sichuan Opera *Tan Ji Er* by Zhang Jun-qiu who acted as Tan Ji-er. His performance in this play proved that he had attained the highest degree of perfection in aria,the inside [Si Ping tune], [Erhuang Yaoban Zhuan San Yan、Yuan Ban], [Nan Bang Zi] and [Er Liu Plate]singing makes you feel that you have once heard of it but everything is fresh and new . It quickly became popular. This play establisheds Zhang School's status in the circle of Peking Opera.

在戏曲影片《望江亭》中饰谭记儿,刘雪涛饰白士中(1958)

In the opera-style film *Riverside Pavilion* as Tan Ji-er , Liu Xue-tao as Bai Shi-zhong (1958).

①

②

③

④

① 《望江亭》中饰谭记儿，刘雪涛饰白士中（1959）
In *Riverside Pavilion* as Tan Ji-er, Liu Xue-tao as Bai Shi-zhong (1959).

② 《望江亭》中饰谭记儿（1978）
In *Riverside Pavilion* as Tan Ji-er (1978).

③ 张君秋演出《望江亭》时使用过的白帔
Baipi (a kind of costume) worn by Zhang Jun-qiu in *Riverside Pavilion*.

④ 《望江亭》中饰谭记儿，刘雪涛饰白士中（1959）
In *Riverside Pavilion* as Tan Ji-er, Liu Xue-tao as Bai Shi-zhong (1959).

在戏曲影片《望江亭》中饰谭记儿,刘雪涛饰白士中(1958)

In the opera-style film *Riverside Pavilion* as Tan Ji-er, Liu Xue-tao as Bai Shi-zhong (1958).

①

②

① 戏曲影片《望江亭》摄制中（1958）
The opera-style film *Riverside Pavilion* was being shot (1958).

② 与戏曲影片《望江亭》摄制组全体合影。前排左起，黄绍芬（摄影师）、张君秋、周峰（导演）、刘雪涛、周伯勋（制片人）（1958）
Having Photo taken with the staff of the opera-style film *Riverside Pavilion*: front row, from left: Huang Shao-fen (photographer), Zhang Jun-qiu and Zhou Feng (directors), Liu Xue-tao and Zhou Bo (production managers)(1958).

诗文会 A Meeting of Poets

　　沈重有女婉娥，欲择佳婿，设诗文会，邀世家子弟顾子玉、牛斯文、车步青会诗。车、牛二人本是纨绔子弟，胸无半点文墨，牛请馆师谢瑛代笔，车请其妹车静芳代笔。会诗结果，牛为首卷，车次之，顾反居末。沈重见牛容貌猥琐，以三卷难分高下为辞，许以金榜高中之后再行议婚。牛斯文慕车步青妹车静芳，欲与之结为连理，车步青代为说亲，车静芳提出以诗文择婿。牛斯文遂请谢瑛代为相亲。诗文会上，车静芳见谢瑛才貌双全，为之心动；谢瑛不忍欺骗车静芳，乃故作歪诗离去。大比之年，谢瑛、顾子玉榜上有名。沈重作主，将女婉娥许配顾子玉，又从中作伐，促成谢瑛、车静芳二人的美满婚姻。

　　张君秋饰演车静芳。在这出戏里，张君秋在［南梆子］、［四平调］的演唱上又有了新的开拓。

　　Shen Zhong intends to choose an ideal husband for his daughter named Wan-e, and a meeting for poets is arranged thereby. Descendants of aristocratic families, Gu Zi-yu, Niu Si-wen, Che Bu-qing are invited to perform their poetry writing technique. Che and Niu are dandies only, knowing no rudiments of writing at all. Niu asks the private school teacher Xie Ying to write on his behalf, while Che asks his younger sister Che Jing-fang to do it. As a result, Niu is on the top of the list, Che is second to him, and Gu turns out to be the last. Finding Niu's ugly looking, Shen Zhong promises to talk about the engagement after the imperial examinations with the excuse that it is hard to distinguish the three papers. Che Si-wen adores Che Bu-qing's sister Che Jing-fang, with an intentim of taking her in marriage. Che Bu-qing, on behalf of him, asks for his sister's attitude. Che Jing-fang proposes to select a prospective mate according to the writing skill. Niu therefore asks Xie Ying to take his place. On the meeting of poets, Che Jing-fang is moved at Xie Ying's appearance and knowledge. Reluctant to deceive Che Jing-fang, Xie Ying leaves with an inelegant verse composed. In the year when the imperial examinations are held, Xie Ying and Gu Zi-yu are on the list of the successful candidates. Sheng Zhong takes his responsibility for the decision: marry his daughter to Gu Zi-yu, and helps to bring about a happy union of Xie Ying and Che Jing-fang.

　　Zhang Jun-qiu acts as Che Jing-fang. In this play, Zhang Jun-qiu's performance in Nan Bang Zi and Si Ping tune improves to a new stage.

《诗文会》中饰车静芳（1959）
In *A Meeting of Poets* as Che Jing-fang (1959).

① 《诗文会》中饰车静芳（1959）
In *A Meeting of Poets* as Che Jing-fang (1959).

② ③ ④ 在戏曲电视片《诗文会》中饰车静芳（1984）
In the opera-style television *A Meeting of Poets* as Che Jing-fang (1984).

【西厢记】 The West Chamber

书生张珙赴长安应试途经博陵，住普救寺。适遇崔相国夫人携女莺莺及子欢郎扶夫柩归博陵，滞留普救寺。张珙游殿遇莺莺，一见倾心，在相国荐亡之日以祭奠亡父为借口，同莺莺侍女红娘搭话，探问莺莺情由。夜晚张珙在西厢墙外抚琴吟诗，莺莺闻听，心生爱慕，遂赋诗唱和。一日，孙飞虎率兵围困普救寺，欲掳莺莺。相国夫人情急，声言如有人能退贼兵愿以小女相许。张珙修书致友杜确发兵解围。事后夫人反悔，设酒宴款待张珙，要张珙与莺莺以兄妹相称。张珙因气急生病，红娘不平，从中传书递笺，成就二人好事。夫人得知，拷问红娘。红娘以实相告，并晓以大义。夫人无奈，乃许婚，并以崔家三代不招白衣女婿为由令张珙长安赴试。莺莺与张珙长亭洒泪分别。张珙落第而归，被崔母逐出，崔莺莺决意相随。夫妻二人并骑出奔。

这是为庆祝建国10周年，由田汉根据明王实甫的名著改编而成的，张君秋同中国京剧院艺术家叶盛兰、杜近芳等合作创演了这个剧目，张君秋饰演崔莺莺。张君秋在这出戏中对京剧的旦角唱腔艺术做了大幅度的创新，正反二黄、正反西皮的各种板式尽在其中，各种板式的起唱以及它们之间的相互转接自然熨贴，行腔之中能够不露痕迹地糅入其他剧种、行当的声腔，随心所欲而不逾矩。由此，使得崔莺莺这一封建社会大家闺秀中的叛逆形象得到了生动的展现。

A young intellectual, Zhang Gong from Luoyang is on his way to Changan, where he is to take the imperial examination. He stays in the west wing of Pujiu Temple. The late Prime Minister's widow Madam Cui and her children make a stop at Puzhou (today's Yongji County, Shanxi Province) and also put up at the Pear Blossom Courtyard guesthouse of the temple, on their way to Changan. When Zhang and Madam Cui's daughter, Ying-ying, meet in the temple hall, the two fall in love. Observing this, Ying-ying's maid Hong-niang commits herself to helping the lovers. Soon after, a mutiny occurs in the local garrison. Hearing of Ying-ying's beauty, the rebel leader besieges Pujiu Temple with the intention of capturing the maiden, at which point her mother, Madam Cui, promises that whoever repels the attackers may have her daughter's hand in marriage. Overjoyed, Zhang immediately writes a letter to his friend Du Que, who arrives with forces strong enough to overwhelm and scatter the rebels. Madam Cui, does not, however, bring up the matter of her promise, and Zhang is so distraught that he falls ill. Feeling deep sympathy for this lovesick young man, Hong-niang persuades her mistress to steal into the garden at midnight and listen as Zhang plays plaintive music to his love on the other side of the wall. Hong-niang later serves as a messenger between Zhang and Ying-ying, and eventually arranges a clandestine meeting for them, when the two plight their troth, flee and spend the following month together. Ying-ying's mother is furious, and severely chastises Hong-niang for her part in the conspiracy. Unfazed, the maid retorts that the young couple had no alternative but to elope, as Madam Cui broke her original promise allowing them to marry. Abashed and speechless, Madam Cui is forced to keep to her original word, but insists that Zhang pass the imperial exam before marrying Ying-ying. Though reluctant to part with his beloved, Zhang sets out for Changan.

This opera, based on Wang Shi-pu's famous work, was adapted by Tian Han for celebrating the 10th anniversary of the founding of People's Republic of China, which was co-operated and co-performed by Zhang Jun-qiu, Ye Sheng-lan and Du Jin-fang from Academy of Chinese Traditional Peking Opera. When Zhang Gong returns without success in the imperial exam, he is driven out by Madam Cui Ying-ying determines to touow Zhang. The couple rides away together.

Zhang Jun-qiu acts as Cui Ying-ying. He innovates greatly on the singing skill of the Dan role in this opera. Various singing modes of the two types of Er Huang and Xi Pi are fully presented in it. The starting methods of the various modes and the switches between them are natural and smooth, in which the tunes of other genres of drama are blended without any noticeable traces. Therefore, the character of Cui Ying-ying, a well-bred girl and rebel against the feudal society is vividly presented before audiences.

《西厢记》中饰崔莺莺
In *The West Chamber* as Cui Ying-ying.

①

②

① 崔莺莺（张君秋饰）课弟欢郎（于淑敏饰），红娘（赵乃华饰）从旁伺候（1979）
Cui Ying-ying (Zhang Jun-qiu) was teaching her brother Huan-lang (Yu Shu-min) a lesson, with Hong Niang (Zhao Nai-hua) waiting beside (1979).

② 张珙（刘雪涛饰）普救寺内巧遇崔莺莺，一见倾心（1979）
Zhang Gong(Liu Xue-tao) fell in love with Cui Ying-ying at the first sight in Pujiu Temple. (1979).

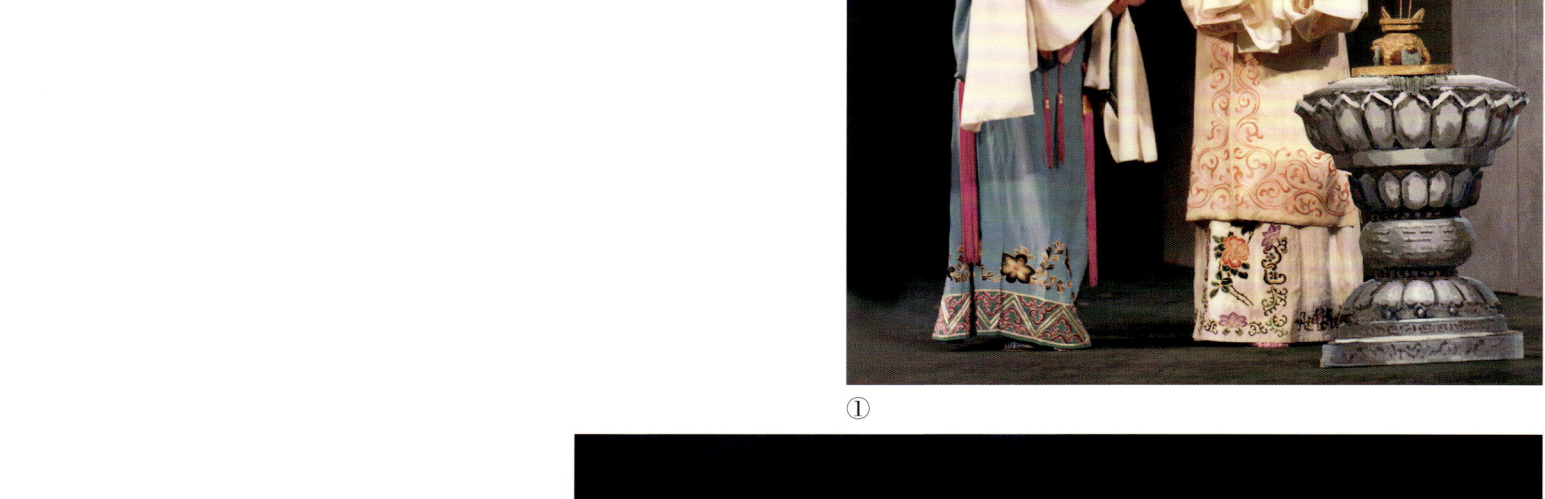

① "凄凉萧寺春将晚，宝香三瓣祝平安。"（1979）
"Miserable Xiao Temple sees the late spring, incense is burnt to express safety" (1979).

② "如何临皓魄，不见月中人。" 张珙隔墙吟诗；"料得高吟者，应怜长叹人。" 崔莺莺隔墙酬韵（1979）
"Since I have seen the bright moon, why can't I see my lover" Zhang Gong sighed on the other side of the wall; " You can't see me but can hear my voice; I am also eager to see you" Cui Ying-ying responded (1979).

③ "笔尖儿横扫那半万儿郎。" 孙飞虎兵围普救寺，崔夫人（耿世华饰）以倒陪妆奁嫁女求救，张珙自荐退兵之策（1979）
"My words will drive away the thousands of soldiers."Sun Fei-hu and his soldiers circled Pu Jiu Temple. Cui Ying-ying's mother (Geng Shi-hua) asked for help by offering to marry Cui Ying-ying and providing the dowry; Zhang Gong volunteered to propose a plan for repulsing the enemy (1979).

① "听红娘一声请梦儿惊觉,恰才向碧纱窗下画了双蛾。" 崔莺莺闻张珙到来,在红娘(杜近芳饰)的搀扶下欣然出堂(1959)
"Wake up after hearing the secret sound made by servant girl Hong Niang , and then I drew two moths on the silk window." Cui Ying-ying went out of her room accompanide by Hong Niang (Du Jin-fang) after hearing that Zhang Gong arrived (1959).

② "兄妹虚名误了我,月底西厢变南柯。" 崔夫人悔婚,崔莺莺愤然掷杯(1979)
"Our disguised relationship as brother and sister proved to be useless; it is a wishful thinking that we can marry each other". Cui Ying-ying was so angry that she smashed the cup because her mother repudiated the marriage contract (1979).

①

②

③

④

① "这萧寺何时来巨匠,把一腔哀怨入宫商。" 崔莺莺在红娘(王婉华饰)的陪同下月夜至花园听到隔墙西厢张珙的琴音哀怨(1962)
"When did a great player come here? Sorrow haunts in the playing."Accompanied by Hong Niang(Wang Wan-hua), Cui Ying-ying went to the garden where she could hear the sorrowful sound from the other side of the wall where Zhang Gong was playing the guzheng (1962).

② "红娘扶我绣楼往,犹有余音绕回廊。" 崔莺莺在红娘搀扶下,恋恋不舍地离去(1959)
"Hong Niang accompanied me toward the embroidery building where the sound of guzheng echoed." Supported by Hong Niang by the arm, Cui Ying-ying was reluctant to leave(1959).

③ "且托香盘供明月,看他倩女会王生。" 红娘牵线,崔莺莺西厢赴约(1979)
"Holding the tray to pray below the moon, the beautiful girl meets her Mr. Right." Hong Niang served as the go-between when Cui Ying-ying went to the West Chamber to meet Zhang Gong (1979).

④ 张珙贸然跳墙,崔莺莺含羞赖简(1979)
Zhang Gong rashly jumped over the wall, and Cui Ying-ying shyly stood there(1979).

创新篇

创立张派

①

②

①崔夫人拷问红娘，红娘晓以大义（1979）
Madam Cui severely chastised Hong Niang, who reasoned with her(1979).

②"问晓来谁染得霜林绛？总是离人泪千行。"崔莺莺为张珙赴试长亭送别（1979）
"It is always a dreadful time to see your lover off", Cui Ying-ying wept while saying farewell to Zhang Gong who would head for Chang Ting (1979).

① "斟美酒不由我离情百倍,恨不得与张郎举案齐眉。"(1979)
"The delicious wine cannot console my lovesickness for Zhang Gong," Cui Ying-ying said (1979).

② "我这里青鸾有信频频寄,你休要金榜无名誓不归。"(1979)
"I will write to you every day, and I just want you back as soon as possible even though you fail in the imperial exam." (1979).

① "雁归空有恨,花落不成春。从此兰闺客,应忘肠断人。" 张珙落第被逐,莺莺决意相随(1979)

"Geese return with grudge;Flowers' falling does not make a spring. Friends of mine forget my sorrowful leaving."Zhang Gong was chased out for his failure in the imperial exam; Cui Ying-ying decided to go with him in spite of his poverty (1979).

② "夫妻双双把马上,碧蹄踏破板桥霜。"(1979)

"The couple step up onto the saddle; the frost on the bridge is smashed when they pass by."(1979).

①

②

① 《西厢记》演出前化妆（1979）
Putting on make-up before performing *The West Chamber* (1979).

② 张君秋演《西厢记》所用过的服装
The costume that Zhang Jun-qiu wore in *The West Chamber*.

【状元媒】 Match Made by Scholar Number One

　　宋王携郡主柴眉春潼台狩猎，遇辽将挑宋王下马，并掳去柴郡主。定山王傅龙之子傅彪救宋王脱险，宋王命其救柴郡主。杨延昭救出柴郡主，郡主得知杨即忠良后代，遂以终身相许，并赠以珍珠衫以为信物，告知请八贤王玉成其事。傅彪赶到，杨延昭追杀辽兵，柴郡主由傅彪护送回朝。杨延昭见八贤王以郡主脱险之事相告。八贤王请状元公吕蒙正为媒，向宋王提亲。宋王误认为救郡主之人是傅彪，命八贤王至天波府悔亲。八贤王同情杨延昭，约吕蒙正商量对策，请宋王金殿辨别真假，柴郡主告以实情，宋王始同意柴郡主与杨延昭完婚。

　　这是张君秋与马连良、谭富英合作创演的剧目，张君秋饰演柴郡主。"宫中"一折，[原板]慢唱且有临时转调的处理，别有新意。

Emperor Song takes Prefecture Hostess Chai Mei-chun to hunt at Tong Tai. The former is thrown down from his horse by a Liao general with a lance; the latter is captured. Fu Biao, the son of Fu Long, King Ding-shan rescues Emperor Song from danger, who orders him to save Prefecture Hostess. Yang Yan-zhao rescues Prefecture Hostess Chai, who, while realizing that Yang is the descendant of a loyal family, promises to be his life-long companion and bestows her pearl garment to him as the souvenir. She asks the eighth brother of the emperor to bring about a happy union of them. Fu Biao arrives to accompany Prefecture Hostess Chai back to her place, and Yang Yan-zhao chases after Liao soldiers. Yang Yan-zhao meets the emperor's eighth brother to inform him of Chai's safety, who asks Number One Scholar Lu Meng-zheng to act as the matchmaker to propose a marriage alliance to Emperor Song. Emperor Song mistakes Fu Biao as Chai's savior, and orders the eighth brother to go to Tian Bo Mansion to break his previous marriage alliance. The eighth brother of the emperor shows sympathy on Yang Yan-zhao, so he meets Lu Meng-zheng to discuss about the issue. Emperor Song is asked to identify the real savior at the imperial hall. Prefecture Hostess Chai tells the truth to the emperor, who approves of the marriage of her and Yang Yan-zhao.

　　This opera is co-produced and co-performed by Ma Lian-liang, Tan Fu-ying and Zhang Jun-qiu, who acts as Prefecture Hostess Chai. In the scene of *Bridal Chamber*, Yuan Ban is sung slowly and there are temporary tune changes, which is of much originality.

《状元媒》中饰柴郡主（1962）
In *Match Made by Scholar Number One* as Prefecture Hostess Chai(1962).

①

②

① 《状元媒》中饰柴郡主（1962）
In *Match Made by Scholar Number One* as Prefecture Hostess Chai(1962).

② 《状元媒》中饰柴郡主，谭元寿饰杨延昭（1960）
In *Match Made by Scholar Number One* as Prefecture Hostess Chai, Tan Yuan-shou as Yang Yan-zhao (1960).

《状元媒》中饰柴郡主，刘雪涛饰赵德芳，高宝贤饰吕蒙正（1963）
In *Match Made by Scholar Number One* as Prefecture Hostess Chai, liu Xue-tao as Zhao De-fang, Gao Bao-xian as Lu Meng-zheng (1963).

① 《状元媒》中饰柴郡主（1984）
In *Match Made by Scholar Number One* as Prefecture Hostess Chai(1984).

② 《状元媒》中饰柴郡主，刘雪涛饰赵德芳
In *Match Made by Scholar Number One* as Prefecture Hostess Chai, Liu Xue-tao as Zhao De-fang.

①《状元媒》中饰柴郡主，刘雪涛饰赵德芳，高宝贤饰吕蒙正，刘盛通饰杨令公，谭元寿饰杨延昭，张洪祥饰傅龙，郝庆海饰傅彪，马长礼饰宋王（1963）
In *Match Made by Scholar Number One* as Prefecture Hostess Chai, Liu Xue-tao as Zhao De-fang, Gao Bao-xian as Lu Meng-zheng, Liu Sheng-tong as Yang Ling-gong, Tan Yuan-shou as Yang Yan-zhao, Zhang Hong-xiang as Fu Long, Hao Qing-hai as Fu Biao, Ma Chang-li as Emperor Song(1963).

② 张君秋演出《状元媒》使用过的服装
The costume that Zhang Jun-qiu wore in *Match Made by Scholar Number One*.

《状元媒》中饰柴郡主，刘雪涛饰赵德芳，张学津饰吕蒙正，高宝贤饰宋王（1986）
In *Match Made by Scholar Number One* as Prefecture Hostess Chai, Liu Xue-tao as Zhao De-fang, Zhang Xue-jin as Lu Meng-zheng, Gao Bao-xian as Emperor Song(1986).

创新篇 — 创立张派

【秋瑾】 Qiu Jin

清末，绍兴女子秋瑾见洋人欺凌百姓，愤而参加革命，鼓吹妇女解放，又以办学堂为名，约定革命党人徐锡麟共同举事，因叛徒出卖而被捕，清廷知府贵福严刑逼供，秋瑾宁死不屈，就义前写"秋风秋雨愁煞人"诗句而死。

这是张君秋创演的一出近代题材的剧目，张君秋饰演秋瑾。内中[高拨子]唱段为京剧传统戏中旦行所不多见。

At the end of Qing Dynasty, Qiu Jin, a Shaoxing lady joined the revolutionary ranks out of indignation after seeing foreigners bully and humiliate the Chinese ordinary people. She advocated women's liberation and in the name of founding schools she proposed a rebel together with the revolutionist Xu Xi-lin. She was captured because of the traitor's betrayal. The Qing Court governor Gui Fu extorted a confession by cruel torture. Qiu Jin would rather die than surrender. She composed the verse of "Autumn wind and autumn rain distress people to death" before her death as a martyr.

This drama, produced and acted by Zhang Jun-qiu, is on a contemporary subject, where Zhang Jun-qiu acts as Qiu Jin. Gao Bo Zi, rarely practised by the Dan role in the traditional Peking Opera, is observed in this one.

①

②

①②《秋瑾》中饰秋瑾（1959）
In *Qiu Jin* as Qiu Jin (1959).

创新篇

创立张派

【秦香莲】 Qin Xiang Lian

陈世美别妻离家赴京赶考，得中状元，被招为驸马。三年后，陈妻秦香莲携子进京寻夫。住在张三元店中，张三元帮助她闯宫见夫，陈世美不念旧情，将秦香莲逐出府门。秦香莲又在宰相王延龄的帮助下，以歌女身份入驸马府拜寿，并唱琵琶词试图打动陈世美。陈不为所动，又命韩棋追杀秦香莲母子，秦香莲告之内情，韩棋放过母子后自杀身亡。秦香莲至开封府状告陈世美，包拯请陈世美过府，劝其悔改。陈世美拒绝认错，包拯不受国太、公主的阻拦，开铡铡了陈世美。

这是张君秋与马连良、谭富英、裘盛戎合作创演的又一个剧目，张君秋饰演秦香莲。在这出戏里张君秋塑造了一个被丈夫抛弃，忍辱负重，在忍无可忍的情况下奋起反抗的古代妇女形象，他在"闯宫"中的[原板]、"祝寿"中的[琵琶词]以及"大堂"中的[哭头]的演唱，生动地传递了秦香莲内心世界的剧烈变化。

Chen Shi-mei leaves his family and wife for the capital to take the imperial examinations, and gains the title of Number One Scholar. He is then taken as the emperor's son-in-law. Three years later, Chen's wife Qin Xiang-lian takes their son and daughter to the capital to look for her husband. She stays in Zhang San-yuan's inn and gets help from Zhang to enter into the palace with difficulty. Unwilling to go back to the past, Chen Shi-mei drives Qin Xiang-lian away from his mansion. With the help of the Prime Minister Wang Yan-ling, Qin enters into Chen's mansion as a singing-girl to offer birthday felicitations. She attempts to move Chen by singing Pi-pa verse. Cold-hearted, Chen orders Han Qi to chase and murder Qin and their children. Being told the truth, Han Qi lets them escape from him and commits suicide. Qin Xiang-lian arrives at the Prefecture of Kaifeng to bring a lawsuit against Chen Shi-mei. Bao Zheng invites Chen to his residence to persuade him to admit his wrongdoings, who flatly rejects it. Regardless of the pressure from the emperor's mother and daughter, Bao decapitates Chen Shi-mei.

This is another opera co-produced and co-performed by Zhang Jun-qiu, Ma Lian-liang, Tan Fu-ying and Qiu Sheng-rong, in which Zhang Jun-qiu acts as Qin Xiang-lian. The character of Qin Xiang-lian is an ancient woman, who is deserted by her husband and suffers from heavy burden physically and spiritually. Unbearable of the maltreatment, she rebels to protect herself. Zhang Jun-qiu's performance in singing Yuan Ban in the scene of *Breaking into the Palace*, Pipa Ci in the scene of *Birthday Celebration*, and Ku Tou in the scene of *Court* vividly conveys the dramatic change in Qin Xiang-lian's inner world.

《秦香莲》中饰秦香莲（1963）
In *Qin Xiang-lian* as Qin Xiang-lian (1963).

① 《秦香莲》中饰秦香莲，马连良饰王延龄（1959）
In *Qin Xiang Lian* as Qin Xiang-lian, Ma Lian-liang as Wang Yan-ling (1959).

② 《秦香莲》中饰秦香莲（1959）
In *Qin Xiang Lian* as Qin Xiang-lian (1959).

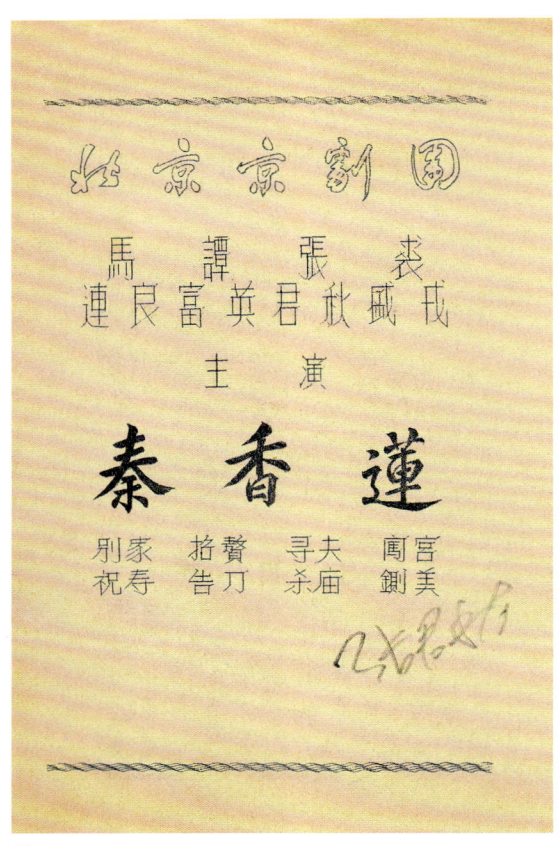

① 《秦香莲》中饰秦香莲，马盛龙饰韩祺，万一英饰冬哥，赵文渝饰秋妹（1959）
In *Qin Xiang Lian* as Qin Xiang-lian, Ma Sheng-long as Han Qi, Wan Yi-ying as Brother Dong, Zhao Wen-yu as Sister Qiu (1959).

② 60年代北京京剧团马连良、谭富英、张君秋、裘盛戎联袂在北京演出《秦香莲》戏单，内有张君秋亲笔签名
The performing list of *Qin Xiang Lian* played by Ma Lian-liang, Tan Fu-ying, Zhang Jun-qiu and Qiu Sheng-rong from Beijing Peking Opera Theatre in 1960s. Zhang Jun-qiu sighed on the performing list.

③ 《秦香莲》中饰秦香莲，裘盛戎饰包拯（1959）
In *Qin Xiang Lian* as Qin Xiang-lian, Qiu Sheng-rong as Bao Zheng (the judge) (1959).

【赵氏孤儿】 The Orphan of Zhao Family

晋灵公无道，建桃花园，以弹击百姓自娱。赵盾闯园进谏，灵公不悦，使屠岸贾几次加害未果。灵公亡，景公立。景公听屠岸贾之言，诛杀赵氏全家。赵盾子赵朔妻庄姬逃入宫中，生下遗孤。屠岸贾闻知，入宫搜孤。门客程婴乔装入宫，救出婴儿。屠岸贾下令全国搜索孤儿，程婴与公孙杵臼计议，以自己的儿子充孤儿托公孙带往其家，而后告发之。公孙与假孤儿被害，屠岸贾收孤儿为子。孤儿长成，程婴为此遭到误解，以至被大将魏绛鞭打。后程婴绘图，向孤儿尽说前情，定计杀屠岸贾，为赵氏报仇。

这是张君秋与马连良、谭富英、裘盛戎合作创演的剧目，张君秋饰演庄姬。张君秋所唱［二黄碰板］、［西皮慢板］等行腔上颇有创新。

Jin Ling-gong, an unprincipled, dim-witted ruler, not only builds a luxurious peach blossom garden, but also takes pleasure in shooting ordinary people. Zhao Dun, the minister, breaks into the garden to offer proposals, which annoys Ling-gong. Zhao Dun is framed by a general named Tu An-jia fruitlessly. Ling-gong dies; Jing-gong ascends the throne. Taking Tu An-jia's words as the fact, Jing-gong intends to kill all members of the Zhao family. Concubine Zhuang, pregnant daughter-in-law of Zhao Dun seeks a shelter in the palace, where she gives birth to a baby. At the message, Tu An-jia enters into the palace to search for the mother and baby. The hanger-on Cheng Ying disguises himself into the palace to rescue the baby. Tu An-jia carries out a nation-wide search for the baby. Cheng Ying discusses with Gongsun Chu-jiu about the issue, reaching an agreement on substituting the orphan with his own son and having him taken to Gong-sun's home. He then reports it to Tu' with Gongsun and the disguised orphan killed. Tu An-jia brings up the baby boy. Cheng Ying is thus misunderstood and whipped by General Wei Jiang when the baby grows up. Later Cheng tells him the whole story by drawing pictures. They plan a revenge to kill Tu An-jia.

This is an opera co-produced and co-performed by Zhang Jun-qiu, Ma Lian-liang, Tan Fu-ying and Qiu Sheng-rong, in which Zhang acts as Concubine Zhuang. Zhang Jun-qiu was creative in using the tune of Erhuang peng plate and Xi Pi slow plate.

《赵氏孤儿》中饰庄姬，马连良饰程婴，刘雪涛饰赵朔，小王玉蓉饰卜凤（1961）
In *The Orphan of Zhao Family* as Concubine Zhuang, Ma Lian-liang as Cheng Ying, Liu Xue-tao as Zhao Shuo, *Junior Wang Yu-rong* as Bu Feng (1961).

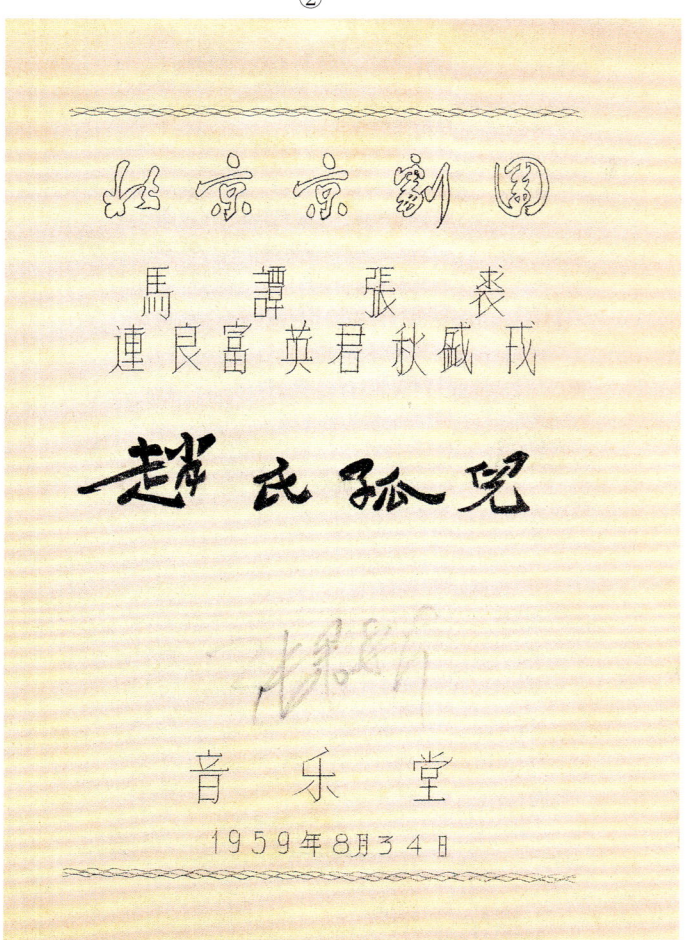

①②《赵氏孤儿》饰庄姬（1961）
In *The Orphan of Zhao Family* as Concubine Zhuang (1961).

③1959年8月3、4日北京京剧团马连良、谭富英、张君秋、裘盛戎在音乐堂联袂演出《赵氏孤儿》戏单，内有张君秋亲笔签名
The performing list of *The Orphan of Zhao Family* played by Ma Lian-liang, Tan Fu-ying, Zhang Jun-qiu and Qiu Sheng-rong from Beijing Peking Opera Theatre on August 3rd and 4th. Zhang Jun-qiu signed on the performing list.

①《赵氏孤儿》中饰庄姬，马连良饰程婴，小王玉蓉饰卜凤（1961）
In *The Orphan of Zhao Family* as Concubine Zhuang, Ma Lian-liang as Cheng Ying, junior Wang Yu-rong as Bu Feng (1961).

②《赵氏孤儿》中饰庄姬，马连良饰程婴（1961）
In *The Orphan of Zhao Family* as Concubine Zhuang, Ma Lian-liang as Cheng Ying (1961).

① 《赵氏孤儿》中饰庄姬，马连良饰程婴，小王玉蓉饰卜凤（1961）
In *The Orphan of Zhao Family* as Concubine Zhuang, Ma Lian-liang as Cheng Ying, junior Wang Yu-rong as Bu Feng (1961).

② 《赵氏孤儿》中饰庄姬（1961）
In *The Orphan of Zhao Family* as Concubine Zhuang (1961).

《赵氏孤儿》中饰庄姬,马连良饰程婴(1961)
In *The Orphan of Zhao Family* as Concubine Zhuang, Ma Lian-liang as Cheng Ying (1961).

【年年有余】 May You Have Excessive Fortune Every Year

某村粮食丰收，在分配方案上颇有争执，生产队长雷老四主张多分；贫协副主席刘金玉是雷家儿媳，她却想到集体储粮备战备荒。正逢公婆为庆寿事意见不一，金玉抓住时机，说服雷老四转变思想。

这是张君秋同马连良合作创演的第一部也是最后一部以现代生活为题材的剧目。

A village has gained a good harvest, but people dispute over the allocation program. The production team leader Lei Lao-si advocates allocating more to villagers; the vice president of the poor peasant association Liu Jin-yu, daughter-in-law of the Lei's, however, considers storing more grains for wars and famines. Taking the opportunity that father-in-law and mother-in-law disagree on the birthday celebration, Jin-yu convinces Lei Lao-si of a change of his thought.

This opera is on a contemporary subject, which is the first as well as the last opera co-produced and co-performed by Zhang Jun-qiu and Ma Lian-liang.

①

①《年年有余》中饰刘金玉（1965）
In *May You Have Excessive Fortune Every Year* as Liu Jin-yu (1965).

②《年年有余》中饰刘金玉，马连良饰雷老四（1965）
In *May You Have Excessive Fortune Every Year* as Liu Jin-yu, Ma Lian-liang as Lei Lao-si (1965).

②

①

②

③

④

① 《芦荡火种》中饰阿庆嫂（1964）
In *Sparks of Reed Marshes* as Sister-in-law Qing (1964).

② 《芦荡火种》中饰阿庆嫂，万一英饰沙奶奶，马长礼饰刁德一，周和桐饰胡传魁（1964）
In *Sparks of Reed Marshes* as Sister-in-law Qing, Wang Yi-ying as Grandmother Sha, Ma Chang-li as Diao De-yi, Zhou He-tong as Hu Chuan-kui (1964).

③ 《芦荡火种》中饰阿庆嫂，刘雪涛饰陈天民，杨少春饰沙七龙，翟韵奎饰刘副官
In *Sparks of Reed Marshes* as Sister-in-law Qing, Liu Xue-tao as Chen Tian-min, Yang Shao-chun as Sha Qi-long, Zhai Yun-kui as Deputy General Liu.

④ 《芦荡火种》中饰阿庆嫂，谭元寿饰郭建光，刘雪涛饰陈天民
In *Sparks of Reed Marshes* as Sister-in-law Qing, Tan Yuan-shou as Guo Jian-guang, Liu Xue-tao as Chen Tian-min.

创新篇

创立张派

望江亭内诗文會
憐香伴侶狀元媒

集余演出四劇目撰聯

七六叟 張君秋

张君秋以四出张派剧目名撰写诗句:"望江亭内诗文会,怜香伴侣状元媒。"
Zhang Jun-qiu composed the poem "A Meeting of Poets in the Riverside Pavilion; A Gentle Companion in the Match Made by Scholar Number One" by borrowing the titles of the four favorite plays of Zhang School.

"文革"之后，张君秋在《加紧培养青年一代是戏曲工作的战略任务》一文中，对"四人帮"造成戏曲队伍青黄不接的现象表示很大的忧虑。他提出，我们戏曲界"应当把培养青年的工作当成一项紧迫的战略任务来抓"。基于这种思想，张君秋把自己的工作重点开始放在了培养青年演员的工作之中。

改革开放以来，张君秋把自己的全部精力投入到教学育人的戏曲教育事业之中。他在中国戏曲学院担任副院长期间，尽心竭力辅导青年教师和学员。他积极参加李瑞环同志倡导的"百日集训"活动，有教无类，为天津市青年京剧团青年演员的成长贡献了自己的力量。他利用出国访问的机会，为海外热爱京剧的学子教学示范，宣传京剧。大江南北，海内海外，张君秋的弟子桃李满天下。

In the wake of the Cultural Revolution, Zhang Jun-qiu, in the article "The Cultivation of the Young Peking Opera Generation is Our Strategic Task", expressed deep concern over the temporary shortage of the Peking Opera talents caused by the "Gang of Four". Meanwhile, he also suggested that the opera circle should place the cultivation of the young Peking Opera talents as one of its pressing strategic tasks. It was based on this thought that he shifted the focus of his work to the cultivation of the young Peking Opera talents.

Since the implementation of the reform and opening up policy, Zhang Jun-qiu devoted all his energy to the undertaking of opera education. As the vice-president of Academy of Chinese Traditional Opera, he did utmost efforts to tutor the young teachers and students there. He also made great contributions to the progress of the performers from Tianjin Young Peking Opera Troupe by actively engaging himself in the 100-day training project advocated by mayor of Tianjin, Comrade Li Rui-huan. He also availed the opportunity of going abroad to promote Peking Opera through teaching the overseas fans. He has students in every nook and cranny of the world.

Education Career 育人篇

菊园耕耘 Cultivation of the Young Generation **襄助"集训"** Indirect Help to the 100-day Training
门墙桃李 A Roomful of Students

菊园耕耘　Cultivation of the Young Generation

　　1979年，张君秋应中国戏曲学院院长史若虚的邀请，担任了中国戏曲学院副院长，把自己工作的重点转移到培养青年一代京剧演员的工作上。任职期间，张君秋尽职尽责，倾尽全力辅导青年教师，提高他们的教学能力，不厌其烦地指点青年学生的表演技巧，循循善诱地引导他们运用京剧的表演艺术手段塑造人物，培养了一批优秀的青年演员。期间，他同曾经与之合作的北京京剧院以及学院的京剧艺术家一道，整理了一批优秀剧目，如《龙凤呈祥》、《苏三起解》、《望江亭》、《西厢记》、《银屏公主》、《状元媒》、《春秋配》等，为青年演员作示范演出。他还在报刊上发表了一系列文章，如《前后三十年》、《我的艺术道路》、《我的少年时代》、《谈京剧流派的继承和发展问题》、《谈戏曲青年演员的学习》、《加紧培养青年一代是戏曲工作的战略任务》、《切忌丢、懒、散》等，以自己的切身体会，鼓励青年演员奋发图强，为京剧事业作出贡献。这些文章集结成书，题名为《张君秋戏剧散论》出版发行。张君秋在戏曲教育事业上的贡献赢得了社会广泛赞誉。1981年6月，张君秋光荣地加入中国共产党。

　　In 1979, Shi Ruo-xu, president of Academy of Chinese Traditional Opera, invited Zhang Jun-qiu to assume the duty of being the vice-president of that institute. Since then, Zhang Jun-qiu began to shift the focus of his work to the cultivation of the young Peking Opera talents. In his term, he fulfilled his duty by doing utmost efforts to tutor young teachers and to improve their teaching ability. He brought up a batch of excellent young performers through patiently guiding them in performing skills and systematically directing them to use the performing artistic approach of Peking Opera to portray figures. It was also in that period that he, together with some of the Peking Opera artists he once cooperated with on the stage from Beijing Peking Opera Theatre and Academy of Chinese Traditional Opera, sorted out a lot of splendid plays for the purpose of teaching and demonstrating, such as *Prosperity Brought by the Dragon and the Phoenix*, *Miss Su San Goes to Trail*, *Riverside Pavilion*, *The West Chamber*, *Princess Yin Ping*, *Match Made by Scholar Number One* and *The Match of Spring and Autumn*. He also made contributions by publishing a series of articles including "Thirty Years", "My Art Road", "My Childhood", "About the Succession and Development of Different Schools of Peking Opera", "The Learning of Drama Young Talents", "The Cultivation of the Young Peking Opera Generation Is Our Strategic Task", "Carelessness, Laziness and Slackness are Taboos", in which he encouraged the young to exert all their strengths to progress by telling his own experiences. All of these articles were put together as a book named "Viewpoints on Opera----Zhang Jun-qiu", which was issued later. His contribution to the undertaking of opera education has won him a universal praise. He became a member of CPC (Communist Party of China) with honor in June 1981.

张君秋（1978）
Zhang Jun-qiu.

①

②

① 与中国戏曲学院院长史若虚在一起（1979）
With President of Academy of Chinese Traditional Opera Shi Ruo-xu (1979).

② "文革"后第一次恢复演出《望江亭》。左起：王幼童、张学敏、王元信、张君秋、刘雪涛、张学济、严元靖、吴吟秋（1978）
The first performance of *Riverside Pavilion* since the Cultural Revolution. From Left: Wang You-tong, Zhang Xue-min, Wang Yuan-xin, Zhang Jun-qiu, Liu Xue-tao, Zhang Xue-ji, Yan Yuan-jing, Wu Yin-qiu (1978).

①

②

③

① 师生同聚一堂。左起，前排：张有荣、苏冬花、孙萍；中排：孙丽英、张君秋、史若虚、蔡英莲、谢虹雯；后排：张蔚、白春香、张静琳、王蓉蓉、杨瑞青（80年代）
Photo of the get-together of masters and their prentices. Front row from left: Zhang You-rong, Su Dong-hua, Sun Ping; middle row: Sun Li-ying, Zhang Jun-qiu, Shi Ruo-xu, Cai Ying-lian, Xie Hong-wen; back row: Zhang Wei, Bai Chun-xiang, Zhang Jing-lin, Wang Rong-rong and Yang Rui-qing(1980s).

② 与中国戏曲学院青年教师艾美君（左二）、谢锐青（右一）等在一起（80年代）
Photo taken with young teachers of Academy of Chinese Traditional Opera. Ai Mei-jun (second left), Xie Rui-qing (first right)(1980s).

③ 为学生示范《玉堂春》（80年代）
Demonstrating *Spring in the Jade Hall* in front of his students (1980s).

① 拜师会（80年代）
The ritual of acknowledging the master (1980s).

② 在拜师会上与弟子们合影。左起第一排：张静琳、杨瑞青、张蔚、王蓉蓉；第二排：谢虹雯、张君秋、刘景毅、张似云；第三排：关静兰、佟娜、黄汝萍、张晓虹、杨淑蕊、蔡英莲、吴香妹（80年代）
Photo taken with prentices on the ritual. First row from left: Zhang Jing-lin, Yang Rui-qing, Zhang Wei, Wang Rong-rong; second row: Xie Hong-wen, Zhang Jun-qiu, Liu Jing-yi, Zhang Si-yun; third row: Guan Jing-lan, Tong Na, Huang Ru-ping, Zhang Xiao-hong, Yang Shu-rui, Cai Ying-lian, Wu Xiang-mei (1980s).

③ 为学生讲授《祭塔》表演（80年代）
Lecturing *A Sacrifice to The Tower* to students(1980s).

①

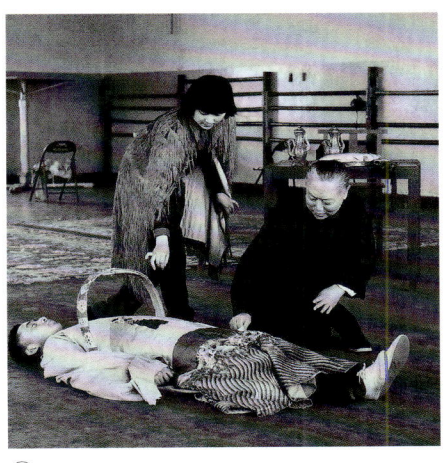

④

②

③

⑤

① 为张静琳（右二）排《望江亭》(1982)
Helping Zhang Jing-lin rehearse *Riverside Pavilion* (1982).

②③④⑤ 为中国戏曲学院学生排《望江亭》(1982)
Helping students of Academy of Chinese Traditional Opera rehearse *Riverside Pavilion* (1982).

② "倒酒"
"Wine serving".

③ "拔剑"
"Pulling out sword".

④ "搜身"
"Frisking".

⑤ 说戏
Instruction of opera.

育人篇

菊园耕耘

①

②

③

④

⑤

⑥

① ② ③ 在中国戏曲学院，同俞振飞为学生作表演示范讲学（80年代）
Demonstrating and lecturing for the students of Academy of Chinese Traditional Opera with Yu Zhen-fei (1980s).

④ 讲学后师生合影（80年代）
Photo taken with students after the lecture (1980s).

⑤ 演出《龙凤呈祥》，由中国戏曲学院青年教师扮演宫女（1982）
Performing *Prosperity Brought by the Dragon and the Phoenix*, the young teachers of Academy of Chinese Traditional Opera as maids of honor. (1982).

⑥ 中国戏曲学院毕业生演出《四郎探母》后，张君秋等领导、专家同学生合影（1981）
After the performance of *Si Lang Visits His Mother* presented by the graduates of Academy of Chinese Traditional Opera, Zhang Jun-qiu and other leaders took photo with them(1981).

①《龙凤呈祥》演出前化妆（1982）
Face-painting before the performance of *Prosperity Brought by the Dragon and the Phoenix*(1982).

②《龙凤呈祥》中饰演孙尚香（1982）
In *Prosperity Brought by the Dragon and the Phoenix* as Sun Shang-xiang(1982).

③《龙凤呈祥》中饰孙尚香，高盛麟饰赵云，李甫春饰刘备（1982）
In *Prosperity Brought by the Dragon and the Phoenix* as Sun Shang-xiang, Gao Sheng-lin as Zhao Yun, Li Pu-chun as Liu Bei(1982).

1981年6月，张君秋同志光荣加入中国共产党
In June 1981, Zhang joined CPC (Communist Party of China) with honor.

④

⑤

⑥

④ 在中国戏曲学院党支部大会上宣读入党申请书
Announcing the application for CPC membership in the party branch meeting in Academy of Chinese Traditional Opera.

⑤ 填写入党志愿书
Filling out the application for CPC membership.

⑥ 与会者对张君秋同志表示热烈祝贺
The party members expressed their congratulations to Zhang Jun-qiu for his joining CPC.

育人篇

菊园耕耘

①

②

③

④

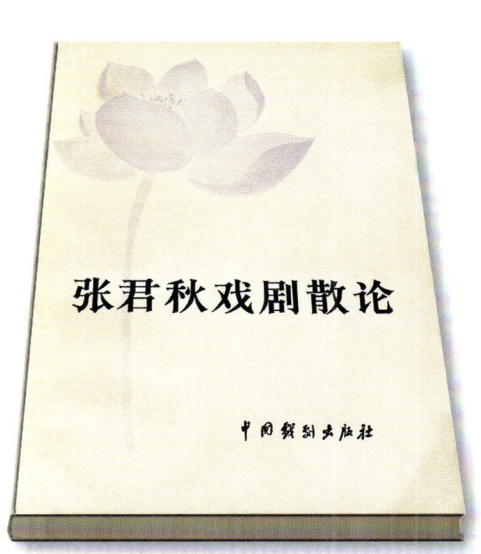

⑥

⑤

① ② 练功
Practicing skills.

③ 吊嗓
Training Voice.

④ 在文化部讲习班上讲学（80年代）
Lecturing in the short-term course organized by the Ministry of Culture (1980s).

⑤ 在座谈会上发言（90年代）
Making a speech in the seminar (1990s).

⑥ 张君秋著作《张君秋戏剧散论》
Zhang Jun-qiu's works: *Viewpoints on Opera-Zhang Jun-qiu*.

① 李瑞环同张君秋谈京剧改革问题。右：张似云（1983）
Li Rui-huan talked with Zhang Jun-qiu on the reform of Peking Opera. Righ: Zhang Si-yun(1983).

② 张君秋在从事戏曲教育事业工作中，还参加社会公益事业。期间，张君秋、张学津父子在"引滦入津"工地慰问演出（1983）
Apart from engaging himself in the education career, Zhang Jun-qiu also played an active role in the public service. Zhang Jun-qiu and his son Zhang Xue-jin performed for the workers of the project of "Luan River to Tianjin Water Diversion" on the building site (1983).

①

②

③

① 1986年，在天津庆祝张君秋舞台生活五十周年活动中，张君秋在《龙凤呈祥》中饰孙尚香，学生们扮宫女。前排左起：徐美玲、张学聪、张静琳、张学华。后排左起：刘明珠、雷英、张晓虹、张君秋、张萍、王蓉蓉、张学敏

In 1986,Tianjin, Zhang Jun-qiu played Sun Shang-xiang and his students played maids of honor in *Prosperity Brought by the Dragon and the Phoenix* for the 50th anniversary since his debut. Front row from left: Xu Mei-ling, Zhang Xue-cong, Zhang Jing-lin, Zhang Xue-hua; Back row from left: Liu Ming-zhu, Lei Ying, Zhang Xiao-hong, Zhang Jun-qiu, Zhang Ping, Wang Rong-rong and Zhang Xue-min.

② 在天津举行的"庆祝京剧表演艺术家张君秋舞台生活五十周年"开幕式上演出《状元媒》，张君秋饰柴郡主，刘雪涛饰八贤王，张学津饰吕蒙正，叶金援饰杨延昭（1986）

In Tianjin, the play of *Match Made by Scholar Number One* was presented on the opening ceremony of the 50th anniversary of Peking Opera artist Zhang Jun-qiu's stage life. Zhang Jun-qiu as Princess chai , Liu Xue-tao as (one of the sons of emperor,) Zhang Xue-jin as Lu Meng-zheng , Ye Jin-yuan as Yang Lan-zhao (1986).

③ 在庆贺张君秋舞台生活五十年活动中与弟子们合影。左起，一排：张静琳、张学聪、张学华；二排：王婉华、张君秋、谢虹雯；三排：蔡英莲、薛亚萍、张萍；四排：雷英、刘明珠、关静兰、孙爱珍、王蓉蓉、杨淑蕊、张晓虹、张学敏、徐美玲（1986）

Photo taken with his prentices on the occasion of the 50th anniversary of his stage life. First row from left: Zhang Jing-lin, Zhang Xue-cong, Zhang Xue-hua; second row: Wang Wan-hua, Zhang Jun-qiu, Xie Hong-wen; third row: Cai Ying-lian, Xue Ya-ping, Zhang Ping; fourth row: Lei Ying, Liu Ming-zhu, Guan Jing-lan, Sun Ai-zhen, Wang Rong-rong, Yang Shu-rui, Zhang Xiao-hong, Zhang Xue-min, Xu Mei-ling (1986).

②

①

③

④

① 1993年在北京举办庆祝"张君秋艺术生活六十周年"活动。刘忠德部长代表文化部向张君秋颁发表彰状："艺高德劭、继往开来"
Celebration activities of the 60th anniversary of Zhang Jun-qiu's stage life were held in Beijing. Minister Liu Zhong-de, representing Ministry of Culture, spoke highly of him: Professionally and morally respected, Zhang Jun-qiu is a person who inherits the past and ushers in the future(1993).

② 文化部常务副部长高占祥讲话
The deputy minister Gao Zhan-xiang of Ministry of Culture addressed a speech.

③ 张君秋在庆祝大会上讲话
Zhang Jun-qiu addressed a speech on the celebration meeting.

④ 演出结束后，张君秋携弟子们谢幕
After performance, Zhang Jun-qiu and his prentices answered a curtain call.

菊园耕耘

①②③④ 张家子女演出《龙凤呈祥》结束后，张君秋同子女等留影（1993）。图中，张学津饰前乔玄后鲁肃，张学济饰周瑜，张学浩饰赵云，张学敏饰孙尚香，张学玲饰吴国太，张学海饰刘备，张学治饰赵云，张学华饰孙尚香，张学江饰孙权，张学沄饰孔明，张学涛饰吕范，张学源饰乔福，张学德饰贾化，王幼童饰张飞，张新饰孙尚香；张学采、张学聪也参加了纪念活动

After the performance of *Prosperity Brought by the Dragon and the Phoenix*, Zhang had a photo taken with his family members (1993). Zhang Xue-jin as Qiao Xuan and later Lu Su, Zhang Xue-ji as Zhou Yu, Zhang Xue-hao as Zhao Yun, Zhang Xue-min as Sun Shang-xiang, Zhang Xue-ling as Wu Guo-tai, Zhang Xue-hai as Liu Bei, Zhang Xue-zhi as Zhao Yun, Zhang Xue-hua as Sun Shang-xiang, Zhang Xue-jiang as Sun Quan, Zhang Xue-yun as Kong Ming, Zhang Xue-tao as Lu Fan, Zhang Xue-yuan as Qiao Fu, Zhang Xue-de as Jia Hua, Wang You-tong as Zhang Fei, Zhang Xin as Sun Shang-xiang; Zhang Xue-cai and Zhang Xue-cong were also in the activities.

张君秋子女演出结束后,张君秋同他的子孙欢聚一堂。右二为刘雪涛(1993)
Zhang Jun-qiu and his family members enjoyed their time after the performance. Second right is Liu Xue-tao (1993).

① 在中央电视台演唱毛泽东诗词《娄山关》(1991)
Singing Mao Ze-dong's poetry *Lou Shan Pass* at China Central Television Station (1991).

② 同弟子们共唱《娄山关》(1993)
Singing Mao Ze-dong's poetry *Lou Shan Pass* with his prentices (1993).

育人篇

菊园耕耘

① 在"纪念徽班晋京二百周年"活动开幕式上，张君秋在观众敬献的花篮前留影（1990）
On the opening ceremony of the 200th anniversary of Anhui Troupes coming to Beijing, Zhang had a photo taken in front of the flower basket offered by audiences (1990).

② 在"纪念徽班晋京二百周年"活动开幕式上，张君秋饰前孙尚香，杨淑蕊饰后孙尚香（1990）
On the opening ceremony of the 200th anniversary of Anhui Troupes coming to Beijing, Zhang Jun-qiu acted as Sun Shang-xiang in the first half, Yang Shu-rui as Sun Shang-xiang in the second half (1990).

③ 参加香港纪念徽班晋京二百周年活动，在中国京剧艺术团记者招待会。左一，谭元寿；右一，杜近芳；右二，梅葆玖（1990）
At the press conference of Chinese Peking Opera Troupe during the 200th anniversary of Anhui Troupes coming to Beijing. Second right: Mei Bao-jiu, first right: Du Jin-fang, first left: Tan Yuan-shou (1990).

襄助"集训" Indirect Help to the 100-day Training

1986年，应李瑞环邀请，张君秋作为艺术总顾问赴天津参加天津市青年京剧团"百日集训"工作。他强调剧团要"一棵菜"，在他亲自指导下，对剧团各个行当的青年演员、乐队演奏员，以至舞台装置、服装道具的工作人员，都悉心指点，严格要求，力求规范，一丝不苟。他以身作则，手把手地传授技艺，还为剧团多方延请名师，因材施教，培养出一批实力雄厚的青年演员。现在，天津市青年京剧团已经成为阵容整齐、行当齐全、流派纷呈的京剧劲旅，在海内外演出获得广泛好评，被新闻媒介誉为"中国京剧之希望"。"百日集训"为培养青年京剧人才提供了可贵的经验。

In 1986, at the invitation of Li Rui-huan, Zhang Jun-qiu, as the senior artistic counselor, went to Tianjin to join in the 100-day training of Tianjin Young Peking Opera Troupe. He emphasized the collectivity of the troupe, which required collective artistic creation. He was strict and tutored in person the young performers of different roles, the performers of band, and the staff in charge of stage settings, costumes and props. And he was scrupulous about every detail in the performing. He also set a good example with his own conducts and passed on his own knowledge and skills. Moreover, he invited well-known masters from different places and suited instruction to a student's level, thus bringing up a batch of excellent young performers. At present, Tianjin Young Peking Opera Troupe has become an outstanding one for its well-balanced cast, complete types of roles and numerous schools. Its performance has won universal praise at home and abroad and is credited, by the press, as the hope of China's Peking Opera. The 100-day training has provided precious experiences for the cultivation of young Peking Opera talents.

"百日集训"期间，同李瑞环在一起
With Li Rui-huan during 100-day training.

① 李瑞环同张君秋、刘雪涛、周文贵、张似云步入天津市青年京剧团排演厅，高兴地说："瞧，我给你们请来多少位好老师！"（1986）
Mayor of Tianjin Li Rui-huan, together with Zhang Jin-qiu, Liu Xue-tao, Zhou Wen-gui, Zhang Si-yun, walked into the rehearsal hall of Tianjin Young Peking Opera Troupe, and said with smile: "Look! I've invited so many excellent artists for you." (1986).

② 谭元寿（右一）、丁存坤（右二）、程正泰（左三）共同收张克（右三）为徒，张君秋偕夫人谢虹雯表示祝贺（1986）
Zhang Jun-qiu and his wife Xie Hong-wen expressed congratulations to Zhang Ke(third right), who became the prentice of Tan Yuan-shou (first right), Jing Cun-kun(second right), and Cheng Zheng-tai(third left) (1986).

③ 集体拜师会上师徒合影。
程正泰、谭元寿、丁存坤（前排左一、二、三）与张克（后排左一）；刘雪涛（前排左四）与许迎生、康健（后排左二、三）；周文贵（前排右三）与蓝文云（后排右三）；郭元祥（前排右二）与石晓亮（后排右二）；茹元俊（前排右一）与王立军（后排右一）（1986）
Photo of masters and their prentices: Cheng Zheng-tai, Tan Yuan-shou, Ding Cun-kun (front row, from left) and their apprentice Zhang Ke (back row, first left); Liu Xue-tao (front row, fourth left) and his prentices Xu Ying-Sheng, Kang Jian (back row, second and third left); Zhou Wen-gui (front row, third right) and his prentice Lan Wen-yun (back row, third right); Guo Yuan-xiang(front row, second right) and his prentice Shi Xiao-liang (back row, second right); Ru Yuan-jun(front row, first right) and his prentice Wang Li-jun(back row, first right) (1986).

①

②

① 李瑞环、张君秋、何顺信（左三）、程正泰（左四）同天津市青年京剧团演员在一起（1986）
With mayor of Tianjin Li Rui-huan and Zhang Jun-qiu the performers of Tianjin Young Peking Opera Troupe: He Shun-xin (third left), Cheng Zheng-tai (fourth left) (1986).

② 李瑞环、张君秋在排演场观看青年演员排戏（1986）
Li Rui-huan and Zhang Jun-qiu looked at the rehearsal of the young performers (1986).

① ② ③ 为雷英、孟广禄、张克说戏
Discussing with Lei Ying, Meng Guang-lu and Zhang Ke.

"百日集训"后,天津市青年京剧团一批演员茁壮成长,积累了一批剧目

After the 100-day training course, a batch of young performers of Tianjin Young Peking Opera Troupe were able to perform better and many works were accumulated.

① 《英雄义》王立军饰史文恭
In *The Loyalty of Heroes*, Wang li-jun as Shi Wen-gong.

② 《锁五龙》孟广禄饰单雄信
In *Locking Five Dragons*, Meng Guang-lu as Shan Xiong-xin.

③ 《红鬃烈马》张克饰薛平贵
In *High-Spirited Horses with Long Hair*, Zheng Ke as Xue Ping-gui.

④ 《金山寺、断桥、雷峰塔》赵秀君饰白素贞
In *Jin Shan Buddhist Temple, Broken Bridge, Lei Feng Pagoda*, Zhao Xiu-jun as Bai Su-zhen.

①

②

③

④

①《竹林计》李佩红饰刘金定
In *A Tale of Bamboos*, Li Pei-hong as Liu Jin-ding.

②《六月雪》刘桂娟饰窦娥
In *Snow in June*, Liu Gui-juan as Dou Er.

③《三盗九龙杯》石晓亮饰杨香武
In *Stealing the Nine Dragon Cup Three Times*, Shi Xiao-liang as Yang Xiang-wu.

④《游六殿》蓝文云饰刘清提
In *Touring Six Palaces*, Lan Wen-yu as Liu Qing-ti.

①

②

① 李瑞环同志和中共中央政治局委员、天津市委书记张立昌（前右五），与天津市其他领导李盛霖（前右三）、房凤友（前左五）、宋平顺（前左三）、刘峰岩（前右一）、刘胜玉（前左一）等观看天津市青年京剧团演出《楚宫恨》后与演员的合影

After seeing the revised representative play of Zhang School *The Story in the Palace of Chu*, Li Rui-huan, Zhang Li-chang (Front row, fifth right), who is the member of the Political Bureau of the CPC Central Committee and Party Secretary of Tianjin municipality, and other municipal leaders Li Sheng-lin (front row, third right), Fang Feng-you (front row, fifth left), Song Ping-shun (front row, fifth left), Liu Feng-yan (front row, fifth right), and Liu Sheng-yu (front row, fifth) left took photo with the performers from Tianjin Young Peking Opera Troupe.

② 天津市青年京剧团演出《秦香莲》剧照。赵秀君饰秦香莲，孟广禄饰包拯，马连生饰陈世美

Photo of play *Qin Xiang Lian* presented by Tianjin Young Peking Opera Troupe. Zhao Xiu-jun as Qin Xiang-lian, Meng Guang-lu as Bao Zhen, Ma Lian-sheng as Chen Shi-mei.

门墙桃李　A Roomful of Students

张君秋的艺术受到青年演员的倾慕，向他拜师求艺以及登门请益者遍及海内外。许多张派弟子都成为所在剧团的顶梁柱，深受观众喜爱。如山东省京剧院的薛亚萍，北京京剧院的杨淑蕊、关静兰和时下当红的王蓉蓉，北京军区政治部战友京剧团的张萍，山东烟台京剧团的董翠娜，天津市青年京剧团的赵秀君，天津京剧院的张学敏等。中国戏剧学院教授蔡英莲在她的教学工作中，悉心传授张派艺术，为张派艺术的传承做了许多工作。张派再传子弟也不断涌现，其中上海京剧院的赵群和天津京剧院实验京剧团的姜亦珊等，引起观众的殷切关注。

Zhang Jun-qiu was greatly admired by many young performers due to his achievements in art, and those who wanted to acknowledge him as master or call at his house for advice scattered around the world. Many of his students have become the backbones of different troupes: Xue Ya-ping from Peking Opera Theatre of Shandong Province, Yang Shu-rui, Guan Jing-lan and currently popular Wang Rong-rong from Beijing Peking Opera Theatre, Zhao Xiu-Jun from Tianjin Young Peking Opera Troupe, Zhang Ping from Military Area Political Department Comrade Beijing Opera Troupe, Dong Cui Na from peking Opera Troupe of shandong Yan Tai. Zhang Xue-min from Tianjin Peking Opera Theatre, etc. Professor Cai Ying-Lian from Academy of Chinese Traditional Opera has also devoted all her attention in carrying on the Zhang School in teaching. Successors of "Zhang School" emerge constantly, particularly Zhao Qun from Shanghai Peking Opera Theatre and Jiang Yi-Shan from the Experimental troupe of Tianjin Peking Opera Theatre have drawn great attention from audiences.

桃李满天下
Having students in every nook and cranny of the world.

① 薛亚萍（后排居中）拜张君秋为师留影（1962）
Photo taken with his prentice Xue Ya-ping (1962).

② 薛亚萍在《状元媒》中饰柴郡主
Xue Ya-ping as Princess Chai in *Match Made by Scholar Number One*.

③ 薛亚萍在《望江亭》中饰谭记儿
Xue Ya-ping as Tan Ji-er in *Riverside Pavilion*.

育人篇

门墙桃李

①

②

③

④

⑤

⑥

① 张君秋、杨淑蕊师生合影
Zhang Jun-qiu and his prentice Yang Shu-rui.

② 杨淑蕊在《四郎探母》中饰铁镜公主
Yang Shu-rui as Princess Tie Jing in *Si Lang Visits His Mother*.

③ 杨淑蕊在《诗文会》中饰车静芳
Yang Shu-rui as Che Jing-fang in *A Meeting of Poets*.

④ 张君秋向蔡英莲授艺
Zhang Jun-qiu imparted skills to Cai Ying-lian.

⑤ 戏曲影片《诗文会》中，张君秋饰车静芳，蔡英莲饰沈婉娥
Zhang Jun-qiu as Che Jing-fang, Cai Ying-lian as Shen Wan-er in opera-style film *A Meeting of Poets*.

⑥ 蔡英莲与张派再传弟子
Cai Ying-lian and her prentices.

① 张君秋、王蓉蓉师生合影
Photo taken with his prentice Wang Rong-rong.

② 王蓉蓉在《四郎探母》中饰铁镜公主
Wang Rong-rong as Princess Tie Jing in *Si Lang Visits His Mother*.

③ 王蓉蓉在《西厢记》中饰崔莺莺
Wang Rong-rong as Cui Ying-ying in *The West Chamber*.

育人篇

门墙桃李

① 张君秋、董翠娜师生合影
Having photo taken with his prentice Dong Cui-na.

② 董翠娜在《秋瑾》中饰秋瑾
Dong Cui-na as Qiu Jin in *Qiu Jin*.

③ 董翠娜在《祭塔》中饰白素贞
Dong Cui-na as Bai Su-zhen in *A Sacrifice to The Tower*.

育人篇

门墙桃李

①

②

③

① 张君秋、张萍师生合影
Photo taken with his prentice Zhang Ping.

② 张萍在《西厢记》中饰崔莺莺
Zhang Ping as Cui Ying-ying in *The West Cnamber*.

③ 张萍在《楚宫恨》中饰马昭仪
Zhang Pin as Ma Zhao-yi in *The Story in the Palace of Chu*.

④ 张君秋、赵秀君师生合影
Photo taken with his prentice Zhao Xiu-jun.

⑤ 赵秀君在《刘兰芝》中饰刘兰芝
Zhao Xiu-jun in *Liu Lan Zhi* as Liu Lan-zhi.

⑥ 赵秀君在《韩玉娘》中饰韩玉娘
Zhao Xiu-jun in *Han Yu Niang* as Han Yu-niang.

育人篇

门墙桃李

②

③

①

① 张君秋、关静兰师生合影
Photo of Zhang Jun-qiu and his prentice Guan Jing-lan.

② 关静兰在《四郎探母》中饰铁镜公主
Guang Jing-lan as Princess Tie Jing in *Si Lang Visits His Mother*.

③ 关静兰在《西厢记》中饰崔莺莺
Guang Jing-lan as Cui Ying-ying in *The West Chamber*.

④ 张君秋、张学敏师生合影
Photo taken with his prentice Zhang Xue-min.

⑤ 张学敏在《起解》中饰苏三
Zhang Xue-min as Su San in *Miss Su San Goes to Trial*.

⑥ 张学敏在《望江亭》中饰谭记儿
Zhang Xue-min as Tan Ji-er in *Riverside Pavilion*.

育人篇

门墙桃李

① 赵群
Zhao Qun.

② 赵群在《二进宫》中饰李艳妃
Zhao Qun as Concubine Li Yan in *Entering Palace for a Second Time*.

③ 姜亦珊
Jiang Yi-shan.

④ 姜亦珊在《四郎探母》中饰铁镜公主
Jiang Yi-shan as Princess Tie Jing in *Si Lang Visits His Mother*.

张君秋辅导学生主张"广开门路"。他说:"你是我的学生,我鼓励你不仅学演我的戏,也要去学其他流派艺术;不是我的学生,你要肯学我的剧目,我也愿意把自己的一点东西贡献出去;我还愿意把我所知道的其他流派的艺术讲给青年同志。我想,一个青年演员,多学各种流派艺术的长处,再加上自己的所长,艺术的表演本领就会愈来愈强,我们的各种流派艺术才能得到真正的继承和发展。"这是他一贯的思想。40年代,张君秋曾为正在上海戏剧学校学戏的"正"字科学生顾正秋传授尚派剧目《汉明妃》。60年代初,张君秋曾收杨秋玲、杨春霞、李炳淑、李玉芙等兼学各种流派艺术的青年演员为弟子。一些知名艺术家,如刘秀荣、刘长瑜、孙毓敏、李维康、齐淑芳等,虽没有拜过张君秋,但也时常登门求教,张君秋则是有问必答,热心指点。

Zhang Jun-qiu advocated his students to be open to different schools. He said, " If you are my student, I will encourage you to learn from other schools; if you are not, you are also welcome to learn my school. I am also willing to share my knowledge of other schools with the young performers. In my opinion, only when a young performer learns from the advantages of other schools rather than limit himself to its school will he be able to improve, then the succession and development of various schools can be carried on." The above was what he has been advocating. In 1940s, he tutored Gu Zheng-qiu who was studying *Wang Zhao-jun's Marriage*, the representative play of Shang School, at Shanghai Theatre Academy. In the early years of 1960s, he became the master of Yang Qiu-ling, Yang Chun-xia, Li Bing-shu and Li Yu-fu, the young performers who were willing to learn the art of different schools. Some well-known artists, like Liu Xiu-rong, Liu Chang-yu, Sun Yu-min, Li Wei-kang and Qi Shu-fang, though they were not Zhang Jun-qiu's students, often called on his house for advice. The warm-hearted Zhang answered their questions patiently.

①

杨秋玲拜师张君秋仪式后合影。左起:谭元寿、李慕良、马富禄、马连良、张君秋、李世济、杨秋玲、孙岳
Photo taken with his prentice Yang Qiu-ling. From left: Tan Yuan-shou, Li Mu-liang, Ma Fu-lu, Ma Lian-liang, Zhang Jun-qiu, Li Shi-ji, Yang Qiu-ling and Sun Yue.

① 杨秋玲在《红灯照》中饰林黑娘
Yang Qiu-ling as Lin Hei-niang in *Legend of Red Lantern*.

育人篇

门墙桃李

①

②

③

④

① 同杨春霞
With Yang Chun-xia.

② 杨春霞在《桃花扇》中饰李香君
Yang Chun-xia as Li Xiang-jun in *Fan of Peach Flowers*.

③ 李炳淑
Li Bing-shu.

④ 李炳淑在《宇宙锋》中饰赵艳蓉
Li Bing-shu as Zhao Yan-rong in *Top of the Universe*.

育人篇 门墙桃李

① 同李玉芙
With Li Yu-fu.

② 李玉芙在《东方夫人》中饰东方明珠
Li Yu-fu as Oriental Bright Pearl in *Lady from East*.

附：张派弟子及受益者名单

北京

刘秀荣、杨秋玲、刘长瑜、孙毓敏、李维康、李玉芙、夏美珍、沙淑英、吴吟秋、张丽敏、黄汝宜、黄汝萍、温如华、杨淑蕊、关静兰、阎桂祥、蔡英莲、王蓉蓉、张静琳、徐美玲、莫宣、萧香生、冯百葵、赵文渝、刘雅明、张文英、张丽雯、孙丽英、杨瑞青、孙萍、吴香妹、冯月茹、张学敏、卢山、张学聪、张学华、杨永述、李晓兰、张丽媛、李松岩、李红梅、刘峥、王润菁、常叶青、黄菊、秦岩

上海

杨春霞、李炳淑、齐淑芳、朱玲妹、李长华、袁英明、陈小燕、李占华、孙爱珍、王之颖、赵群

天津

季小兰、李近秋、王晶玉、张芝兰、张秀琳、张学敏、刘明珠、雷英、赵秀君、张恩茹、姜亦珊、张蕊麟

山东

薛亚萍、朱晋玲、程青、董翠娜、张萍、翟萍、李淑兰、鲁霞、齐伟、李菁、王雅娜、李芸香、张双捷

山西 曹佛生

湖北

王婉华、陈瑶华、彭泽林、李春芳、邹永华、侯盛梅、方晓慧

河北

宋玉珍、张学秋、王丽华、刘萍、杨玉洁、霍学荣

河南 王蕴芳、佟娜、李如华

辽宁

钟萍、华琳、高小鹏、张丽敏、李鸿坤、马中月、陈美英、唐润之

黑龙江

郭正秋、潘银霞、王金娥、王红、庞盈侠、林桂兰、马莲、高月琴、韩婉齐

江苏 赵静

浙江 李瑛、王小军

湖南 罗小燕

福建 李兰荪、姜淑芸

云南 刘美娟、董汝楠、吉晶

贵州 王晓虹

四川 何淑祥、尹桂梅

内蒙古自治区 曹毅林

新疆 陈瑛

青海 吴玉萍

香港 王晓湖

台湾 顾正秋、徐露、阎兰静、李忆萍、刘海苑

美国

郑丽波、吴爱理、张曼、杨陈洁如、庄陈碧如、谢竹君、刘瑛、计隐、刘宇文、顾剑霞、叶李钰、曹复莲、钟维娜、任月娥、陈关月、安娜、蓝兰

加拿大 章宝明

Attached: Zhang School Students and the People Who Benefited from Him

Beijing

LiuXiu-rong, Yang Qiu-ling, Liu Chang-yu, Sun Yu-min, Li Wei-kang Li Yu-fu, Xia Mei-zhen, Sha Shu-ying, Wu Yin-qiu, Zhang Li-min, Huang Ru-yi, Huang Ru-ping, Wen Ru-hua, Yang Shu-rui, Guan Jing-lan, Yan Gui-xiang, Cai Ying-lian, Wang Rong-rong, Zhang Jing-lin, Xu Mei-ling, Mo Xuan, Xiao Xiang-sheng, Feng Bai-kui, Zhao Wen-yu, Liu Ya-ming, Zhang Wen-ying, Zhang Li-wen, Sun Li-ying, Yang Rui-qing, Sun Ping, Wu Xiang-mei, Feng Yue-ru, Zhang Xue-min, Lu Shan, Zhang Xue-cong, Zhang Xue-hua, Yang Yong-shu, Li Xiao-lan, Zhang Li-yuan, Li Song-yan, Li Hong-mei, Liu Zheng, Wang Run-jing, Chang Ye-qing, Huang Ju, Qin Yan.

Shanghai

Yang Chun-xia, Li Bing-shu, Qi Shu-fang, Zhu Ling-mei, Li Chang-hua, Yuan Ying-ming, Chen Xiao-yan, Li Zhan-hua, Sun Ai-zhen, Wang Zhi-ying, Zhao Qun.

Tianjin

Ji Xiao-lan, Li Jin-qiu, Wang Jing-yu, Zhang Zhi-lan, Zhang Xiu-lin, Zhang Xue-min, Liu Ming-zhu, Lei Ying, Zhao Xiu-jun, Zhang En-ru, Jiang Yi-shan, Zhang Rui-lin.

Shandong

Xue Ya-ping, Zhu Jin-ling, Cheng Qing, Dong Cui-na, Zhang Ping, Zhai Ping, Li Shu-lan, Lu Xia, Qi Wei, Li Qing, Wang Ya-na, Li Yun-xiang, Zhang Shuang-jie.

Shanxi
Cao Fu-sheng.

Hubei

Wang Wan-hua, Chen Yao-hua, Peng Ze-lin, Li Chun-fang, Zhou Yong-hua, Hou Sheng-mei, Fang Xiao-hui.

Hebei

Song Yu-zhen, Zhang Xue-qiu, Wang Li-hua, Liu Ping, Yang Yu-jie, Huo Xue-rong.

Henan

Wang Yun-fang, Tong Na, Li Ru-hua.

Liaoning

Zhong Ping, Hua Lin, Gao Xiao-peng, Zhang Li-min, Li Hong-kun, Ma Zhong-yue, Chen Mei-ying, Tang Run-zhi.

Heilongjiang

Guo Zheng-qiu, Pan Yin-xia, Wang Jin-e, Wang Hong, Pang Ying-xia, Lin Gui-lan, Ma Lian, Gao Yue-qin, Han Wan-qi.

Jiangsu
Zhao Jing.

Zhenjiang
Li Ying, Wang Xiao-jun.

Hunan
Luo Xiao-yan.

Fujian
Li Lan-sun, Jiang Shu-yun.

Yunnan
Liu Mei-juan, Dong Ru-nan, Ji Jing.

Guizhou
Wang Xiao-hong.

Sichuan
He Shu-xiang, Yi Gui-mei.

Nei Menggu
Cao Yi-lin.

Xinjiang
Chen Ying.

Qinghai
Wu Yu-ping.

Hong Kong
Wang Xiao-hu.

Taiwan

Gu Zheng-qiu, Xu Lu, Yan Lan-jing, Li Yi-ping, Liu Hai-yuan.

America

Zheng Li-bo, Wu Ai-li, Zhang Man, Yang Chen Jie-ru, Zhuang Chen Bi-ru, Xie Zhu-jun, Liu Ying, Ji Yin, Liu Yu-Wen, Gu Jian-xia, Ye Li-yu, Cao Fu-lian, Zhong Wei-na, Ren Yue-e, Chen Guan-yue, An Na, Lan Lan.

Canada
Zhang Bao-ming.

《中国京剧音配像精粹》是李瑞环同志创意策划并组织实施的重大文化工程。1994年，张君秋接受李瑞环的委托，担负起音配像工程艺术总顾问的工作，他与京剧界诸多名家一起，充分发挥艺术造诣精湛、舞台经验丰富的优势，满腔热情地投入到这项对于京剧具有深远意义和十分复杂艰巨的工作之中。他以年逾古稀的高龄，曾有严重疾患的抱病之躯，夜以继日，呕心沥血，不遗余力，一直工作到逝世。

"Peking Opera Audio-videotaped Classics" was a grand cultural project masterminded and organized by Comrade Li Rui-huan. In 1994, consigned by Li Rui-huan, Zhang Jun-qiu worked as the chief counselor of "Peking Opera Audio-videotaped Classics". Together with many experts of Peking Opera, he devoted himself wholeheartedly to the project that is complex but everlasting with his gorgeous techniques and stage experiences. He had been working hard though he was almost 70 years old with his sick body day and night until the last minute of his life.

Peking Opera Master ZHANG JUNQIU

Achievements of Audio Video Tapes "配像"篇

任重道远 Shouldering Heavy Responsibility **呕心沥血** Working His Heart Out
"配像"丰碑 Imperishable Masterpiece

任重道远 Shouldering Heavy Responsibility

1985年，李瑞环同志在主持天津工作期间，为了振兴京剧，提出京剧精粹音配像的办法。经过十年的探索、试录，在1994年正式启动《中国京剧音配像精粹》工程，并请张君秋担任该工程的艺术总顾问。张君秋深感把当年诸多京剧艺术家的演出原汁原味地用录音配像的形式流传下来，是自己义不容辞的责任，毅然接受了这项工作。

In 1985, as mayor of Tianjin municipality, Li Rui-huan proposed the idea of audio-videotaping Peking Opera Classics for the purpose of revitalizing the undertaking of Peking Opera. After 10 years of trial recording, the project of "Peking Opera Audio-videotaped Classics" was formally launched in 1994, and Zhang Jun-qiu was invited to assume the duty of chief counselor of the project. Zhang Jun-qiu regarded it as his own responsibility to keep the performance of the plays of Peking Opera as their original in the form of "Audio Video Tapes".

李瑞环与张君秋等参加《中国京剧音配像精粹》工作的艺术家、工作人员合影（1997.1）
前排左起：谢虹雯、梅葆玖、谭元寿、张君秋、李瑞环、袁世海、刘雪涛、马崇仁、谢国祥、迟金声
第二排左起：刘长江、李世济、王蓉蓉、高宝贤、张学津、李蔷华、杜近芳、叶少兰、张延培
第三排左起：阎德威、王联生、刘怀萱、吴钰璋、张萍、董圆圆、蔡英莲

The photo of Li Rui-huan and the artists and the working staff of the project of "Peking Opera Audio-videotaped Classics" (Jan.1997).
Front row, from left: Xie Hong-wen, Mei Bao-jiu, Tan Yuan-shou, Zhang Jun-qiu, Li Rui-huan, Yuan Shi-hai, Liu Xue-tao, Ma Chong-ren, Xie Guo-xiang, Chi Jin-sheng
Second row, from left: Liu Chang-jiang, Li Shi-ji, Wang Rong-rong, Gao Bao-xian, Zhang Xue-jin, Li Qiang-hua, Du Jin-fang, Ye Shao-lan, Zhang Yan-pei,
Third row, from left: Yan De-wei, Wang Lian-sheng, Liu Huai-xuan, Wu Yu-zhang, Zhang Ping, Dong Yuan-yuan, Cai Ying-lian.

①

① 1995年4月22日，李瑞环到音配像现场视察时，与演职员合影：（自左至右）迟金声、马崇仁、张学海、董翠娜、张羽、李瑞环、张君秋、张学津、兰燗、高宝贤
On April 21st, 1995, Li Rui-huan made inspection in the place where the audio-videotaped project was carried on, and took photo with the staff: (from left to right) Chi Jin-sheng, Ma Chong-ren, Zhang Xue-hai, Dong Cui-na, Zhang Yu, Li Rui-huan, Zhang Jun-qiu, Zhang Xue-jin, Lan Lan, Gao Bao-xian.

②张君秋同天津市中华民族文化促进会原常务副会长谢国祥（右一）在音配像现场指导工作
Zhang Jun-qiu was directing the project of audio-videotaping together with Xie Guo-xiang, former chief vice chairman of Tianjin Chinese National Culture Promotion Association.

②

1996年12月，李瑞环在人民大会堂新疆厅召开京剧音配像工作座谈会，与张君秋、袁世海、李世济等同志交谈

In December, 1996, Chairman Li Rui-huan was convening to discuss audio-videotaping Peking Opera in the Hall of Xinjiang Autonomous Region inside Great Hall of the People. Li Rui-huan was talking with Zhang Jun-qiu, Yuan Shi-hai and Li Shi-ji.

呕心沥血　Working His Heart Out

张君秋在担任《中国京剧音配像精粹》工程艺术总顾问时已年逾古稀，且患有心脏病，但他仍以满腔热情投入到这项工作。从搜集鉴别录音资料，到挑选配像演员，以至聘请名家指导，事必躬亲，精心指导。他还亲临配像现场，指导青年演员学习、排练配像剧目的表演，热心指教，严格要求，与京剧界袁世海、李世济、谭元寿、梅葆玖、杜近芳、刘雪涛、程正泰、叶少兰、孙毓敏、迟金声、马崇仁等名家一起，充分发挥了艺术造诣精湛、舞台经验丰富的优势。工作期间，张君秋的心脏病复发，经过治疗，病情平稳之后，他又忘我地投入到工作之中，直至逝世。

Though pestered by the cardiovascular disease, the aged master Zhang Jun-qiu enthusiastically devoted great effort to the project of "Peking Opera Audio - videotaped Classics". He engaged himself in almost every part from the collection and identification of the materials to the selection of performers, even to the part of inviting famous artists to instruct. He went to the place where the project was carried out to instruct young performers to play and rehearse the audio-videotaped classics, and he was strict and kind to the students. Together with many experts of Peking Opera like Yuan Shi-hai, Li Shi-ji, Tan Yuan-shou, Mei Bao-jiu, Du Jin-fang, Liu Xue-tao, Cheng Zheng-tai, Ye Shao-lan, Sun Yu-min, Chi Jin-sheng and Ma Cong-ren, he fully displayed the advantages in art attainments and stage experiences. He suffered from heart attack when he was at work. After recovery, he once again put himself into the project until his death.

《状元媒》配像时为马长礼、张学津说戏
Teaching Ma Chang-li and Zhang Xue-jin while audiov-iedotaping *Match Made by Scholar Number One*.

① 《刘兰芝》配像时，与刘雪涛对戏
Rehearsing with Liu Xue-tao while audio-videotaping *Liu Lan Zhi*.

② 《审头刺汤》配像时，与张金梁切磋表演
Discussing with Zhang Jin-liang while audio-videotaping *Identifying the Head and Stabbing Tang*.

《女起解》配像现场
The place where *Miss Su San Goes to Trial* was being audio-viedotaped.

台步
Stage walk.

说位置
Talking about where to stand.

"来生变犬马我当报还"
"I feel the kindness and will repay it."

"洪洞县内无有好人"
"There is no good person in Hong Dong County."

"唯有你老爹爹是个大大的好人"
"Only you aged father is good."

《审头刺汤》配像现场
The place where *Identifying the Head and Stabbing Tang* was being audio-videotaped.

公堂
Tribunal.

取剑
Fetching the sword.

刺汤
Stabbing Tang.

《西厢记》配像现场
The place where *The West Chamber* was being audio-videotaped.

为叶少兰说戏
Teaching Ye Shao-lan.

张萍（饰崔莺莺）、董圆圆（饰红娘）为《西厢记》配像
Zhang Ping (as Cui Ying-ying), Dong Yuan-yuan (as Hong Niang) audio-videotaped for *The West Chamber*.

叶少兰（饰张珙）、张萍、董圆圆为《西厢记》配像
Ye Shao-lan (as Zhang Gong), Zhang Ping, Dong Yuan-yuan audio-videotaped for *The West Chamber*.

《四郎探母》配像现场
The place where *Si Lang Visits His Mother* was being audio-videotaped.

"盗令"之一
Dao Ling first.

"盗令"之二
Dao Ling second.

"回令"之一
Hui Ling first.

"回令"之二
Hui Ling second.

《二进宫》配像现场
The place where *Entering the Palace for the Second Time* was being audio-viedotaped.

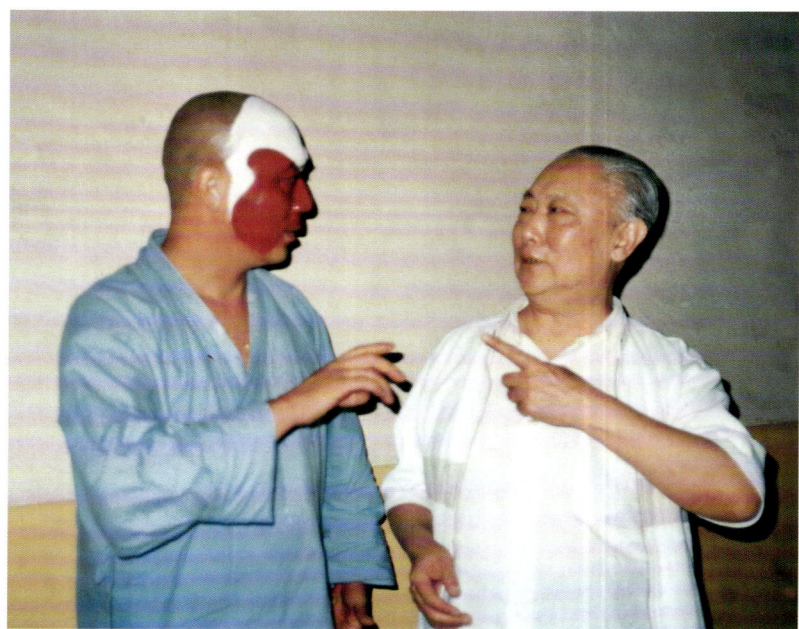

为裘明说戏
Teaching Qiu Ming.

董翠娜（饰李艳妃）、高宝贤（饰杨波）、裘明（饰徐延昭）为《二进宫》配像
Dong Cui-na(as Concubine Li Yan), Gao Bao-xian(as Yang Bo), Qiu Ming(as Xu Yan-shao) audio-videotaped for *Entering the Palace for the Second Time*.

配像完成后
The audio-videotaping work accomplished.

《生死恨》配像现场

The place where *Farewell between Life and Death* was being audio-videotaped.

纺线
Spinning.

举灯
Holding the lantern.

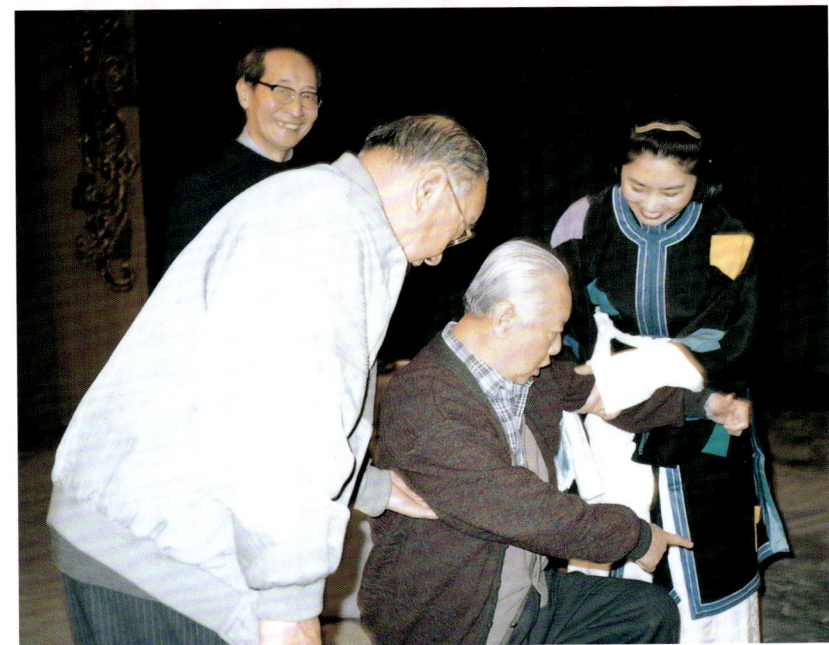

示范
Demonstrating.

同马崇仁（右一）、迟金声（左二）、张萍（饰韩玉娘）
Together with Ma Chong-ren(first right), Chi Jin-sheng(second left), Zhang Ping(as Han Yu-niang).

配像篇
呕心沥血

① 《凤还巢》配像完成后，与梅葆玖（右七）等在一起。
After accomplishing the audio-videotaping work of *The Phoenix Returns to Its Nest*. Zhang was with Mei Bao-jiu (seventh right) and others.

② 在监视器前
In front of the monitoring device.

③ 与电视导演阎德威切磋
Discussing with the TV director Yan De-wei.

指导化妆
Directing how to put on make-up.

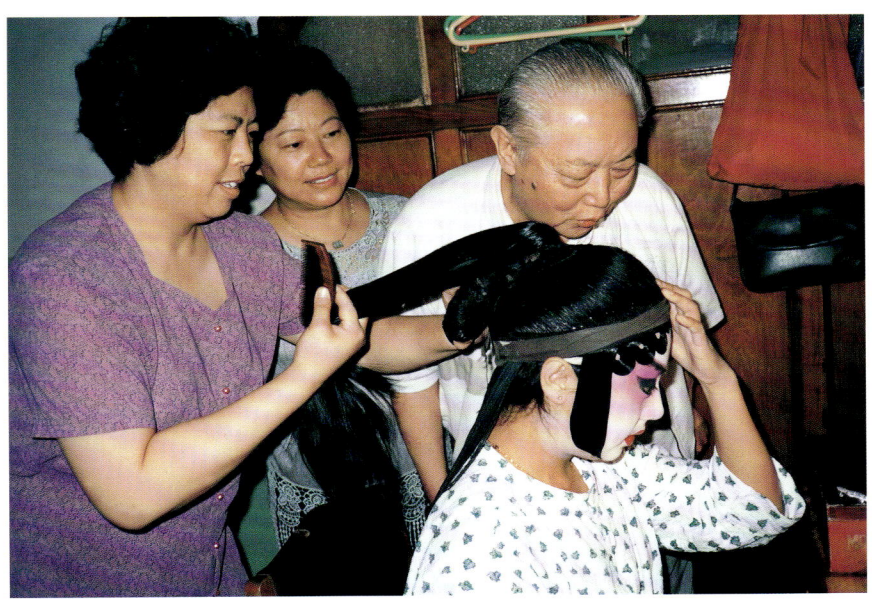

梳头
Combing.

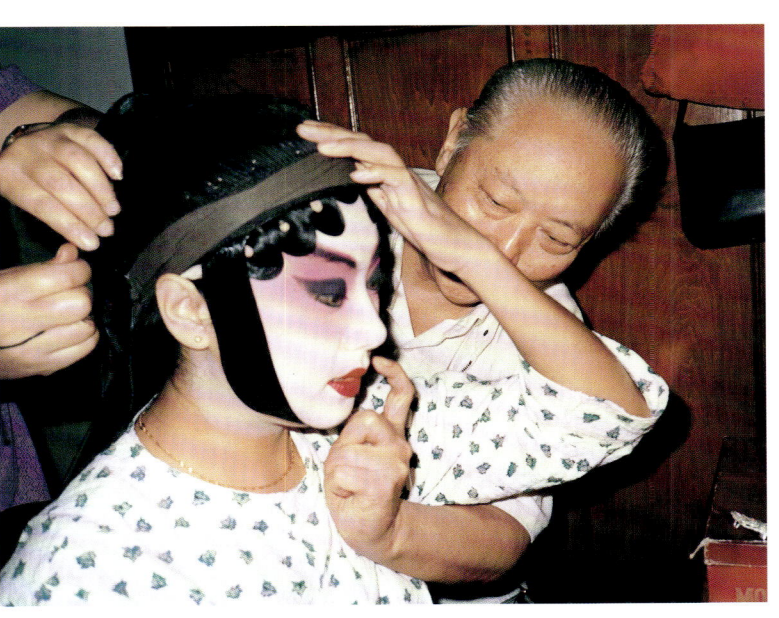

画唇
Putting make-up on the lips.

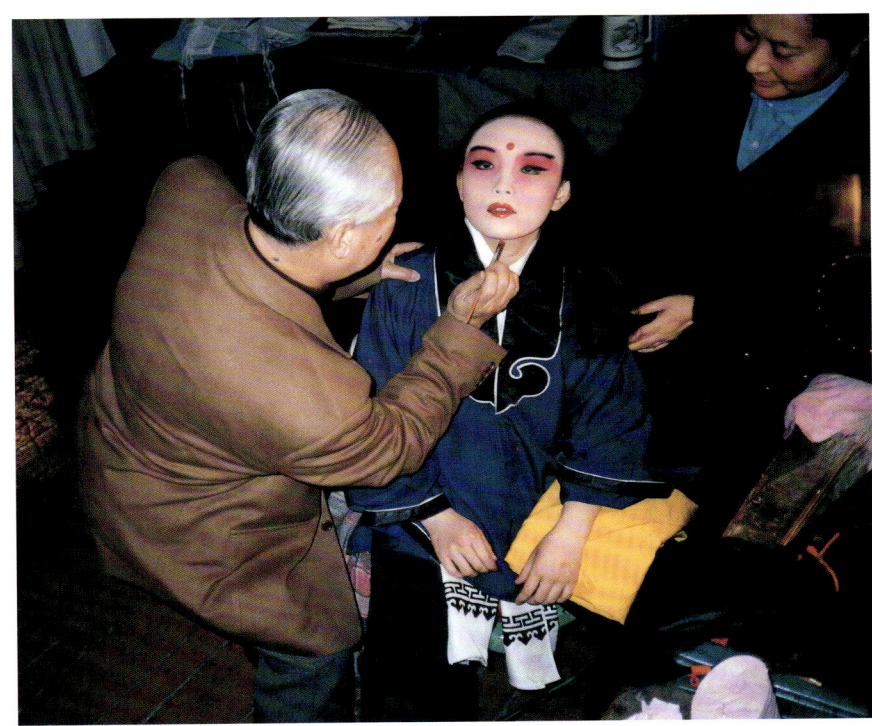

为孙儿张羽配像《三娘教子》薛倚哥化妆
Putting make-up on grandson Zhang Yu who was acting as brother Xue Yi in the audio-videotaped *The Third Mistress Brings Up the Son*.

"自己试试看!"
Try by yourself!

为音配像剧目题写的片头及相关光盘
Written credits for the audio-videotaped play and its related disc.

①

②

③

①张君秋逝世后，他的同事和弟子们继续努力，完成了张派戏的全部录制工作，图为最后一部戏《年年有余》录制结束后，艺术家与工作人员合影。自左至右：董翠娜、张学津、王雁、马崇仁、谢虹雯、刘莉莉、蔡英莲、张萍

Zhang Jun-qiu's colleagues and prentices kept on doing the audio-videotaping and successfully accomplished it after his death. The photo of artists and working staff taken after the audio-videotaping of *Prosperity*. From left to right: Dong Cui-na, Zhang Xue-jin, Wang Yan, Ma Chong-ren, Xie Hong-wen, Liu Li-li, Cai Ying-lian, Zhang Ping.

②《中国京剧音配像精粹》张君秋专集
Peking Opera Audio-videotaped Classics-Zhang Jun-qiu Special Album.

③张君秋影像资料集
Audio-video album of Zhang Jun-qiu.

"配像"丰碑　Imperishable Masterpiece

张君秋在担任《中国京剧音配像精粹》工程艺术总顾问工作的近三年时间里，完成了中国京剧多种流派剧目音配像120部，为观众提供了一批声像并茂、品位较高的京剧欣赏剧目，抢救了不少濒临失传的经典作品，再现了几十名京剧艺术家特别是在"文革"中遭受迫害的老艺术家的成就，训练了一批中青年演员，为振兴、发展京剧艺术做出了巨大贡献，同时为以后的音配像工作奠定了坚实基础。到2002年9月召开《中国京剧音配像精粹》总结会时，共录制出版了355部剧目，同时编辑出版了梅兰芳、尚小云、程砚秋、荀慧生、马连良、谭富英、周信芳、李少春、杨宝森、奚啸伯、张君秋、裘盛戎等24个专集以及《北方鼓曲名家音配像选萃》、《中国评剧音配像》。广大观众和京剧工作者称赞这是一件功在当代利在千秋的文化工程，海外人士和港澳台同胞也给予了高度评价。

张君秋的艺术成就和他对振兴京剧艺术的巨大贡献树起了一座壮丽的丰碑。

During his three years as the chief counselor of "Peking Opera Audio-videotaped classics", Zhang Jun-qiu helped to audio-videotape 120 plays of various schools, thus providing a batch of high-quality Peking Opera plays which offered the audience with excellent images and sound and high taste. He, in this way, saved a lot of almost-lost traditional plays, brought to us the great achievements of many masters of Peking Opera especially those suffered a lot in the Cultural Revolution, and had trained some young performers and made great contribution to the inheritance and development of Peking Opera. Meanwhile, what he did also lays a solid foundation for the audio- videotaping project in the future. In September 2002 when the summing-up meeting of "Peking Opera Audio-videotaped Classics" project was convened, 355 plays had already been recorded and published. Totally 24 special albums respectively of Mei Lan-fang, Shang Xiao-yun, Cheng Yan-qiu, Xun Hui-sheng, Ma Lian-liang, Tan Fu-ying, Zhou Xin-fang, Li Shao-chun, Yang Bao-sen, Xi Xiao-bo, Zhang Jun-qiu, Qiu Sheng-rong and also other products like "Selected Works of Well-Known Artists in Northern China", "Audio-videotaped Works of Pingju Opera" were edited and publised in the meanwhile. Viewers and many Peking Opera artists claim it is a cultural project that benefits for the moment, gains for the millennia, and it has also received high praise from overseas and the compatriots from Hong Kong and Macao.

His artistic accomplishments and his tremendous contribution to the revitalization of Peking Opera are regarded as imperishable masterpieces in the history of Peking Opera.

①

②

③

① 李瑞环讲话
Li Rui-huan gave a speech.

②③《中国京剧音配像精粹》工程总结会会场
Summing-up meeting of the project of "Peking Opera Audio-videotaped Classics".

①

②

①文化部部长孙家正发言
Minister Sun Jia-zheng of Ministry of Culture gave a speech.

②天津市政协副主席、天津市中华民族文化促进会常务副会长叶厚荣发言。
右一为天津市委副书记刘峰岩,左二和左一为香港知名人士张永珍、杨祥波
Ye Hou-rong, vice chairman of Tianjin People's Political Consultative Conference and chief vice chairman of Tianjin Chinese National Culture Promotion Association delivered a speech.
First right: Deputy Party Secretary of Tianjin Municipality Liu Feng-yan; second left: Zhang Yong-zhen; first left: Yang Xiang-bo (both of them are celebrities from Hong Kong).

③老戏剧家马少波发言。右起,一排:马少波、李世济、梅葆玖、叶少兰、马崇仁;二排:冯志孝、杨春霞、高宝贤
Senior dramatist Ma Shao-bo addressed a speech.
First row from right: Ma Shao-bo, Li Shi-ji, Mei Bao-jiu, Ye Shao-lan, Ma Chong-ren; second row: Feng Zhi-xiao, Yang Chun-xia, Gao Bao-xian.

③

①

②

③

④

①京剧名家袁世海发言。前排左起：袁世海、马少波、谭元寿、杜近芳
Famous Peking Opera artist Yuan Shi-hai gave some remarks. Front row, from left: Yuan Shi-hai, Ma Shao-bo, Tan Yuan-shou, Du Jir.-fang.

②舞台导演迟金声发言。右起，前排：迟金声、杜近芳；二排：尚长荣、刘雪涛、张春华、吴素秋
Stage director Chi Jin-sheng gave some remarks. From right, front row: Chi Jin-sheng. Du Jin-fang; back row: Shang Chang-rong, Liu Xue-tao, Zhang Chun-hua, Wu Su-qiu.

③京剧名家叶少兰发言
Famous Peking Opera artist Ye Shao-lan gave some remarks.

④青年演员孟广禄发言
Young performer Meng Guang-lu gave a speech.

①

②

①②为庆祝《中国京剧音配像精粹》总结会召开，在中央电视台举办的《盛世京剧情》专题晚会

Special party named "Prosperous Peking Opera" was held in CCTV to celebrate the summing-up meeting of "Peking Opera Audio-videotaped Classics Project".

蔚为大观——《中国京剧音配像精粹》、《北方鼓曲名家音配像选萃》、《中国评剧音配像》音像制品
Magnificent products----"Peking Opera Audio-videotaped Classics", "Selected Works of Well-Known Artists in Northern China", "Audio-videotaped Works of Pingju Opera".

早在50年代中期，张君秋就创立了张派艺术，他的唱腔不胫而走，
不仅在港、澳、台地区广泛流传，而且飘洋过海，
在美国、日本也吸引了众多戏曲听众，
海内外戏曲观众同张君秋早已心交神往。
改革开放以来，张君秋出访美国、日本，在同新朋旧友的交往结识活动中，
热情宣传京剧，口传心授，乐此不疲，赢得了崇高的声誉。
张君秋的朋友不仅限于戏曲界，
他兴趣广泛，视野开阔，书画、音乐、文学、曲艺等各界，
都有他的良师益友，从这些师友身上，
张君秋汲取了许多宝贵的艺术经验，丰富了自己的艺术。

As early as mid 1950s, Zhang founded his Zhang's school and his aria spread fast and was appreciated by the Peking Opera fans in Hong Kong, Macao and Tai Wan areas. His performance also attracted many westerners who had already become intimate friends with Zhang. Since the implementation of the policy of reform and opening-up, he had been devoting great efforts in promoting Peking Opera, and had won great reputation among the countries he had ever visited such as the United States and Japan. He had friends in various walks such as calligraphy, music, literature and drama, from whom he had learned a great deal of precious artistic experiences, which helped to enrich his arts.

Peking Opera Master
ZHANG JUNQIU

Keeping Companion with Others 交游篇

艺播四海 The Worldwide Spread of His Art 博识多才 Being of Great Learning and Great Ability
良师益友 Mentors 闲情逸趣 Leisurely and Carefree Mood

艺播四海　The Worldwide Spread of His Art

　　1963 年，张君秋等出演香港，盛况空前。此后，他的音像制品更加广泛流传，不仅流传港、澳、台地区，而且艺播四海，美国、日本的许多张派艺术的爱好者学唱、学演张派艺术也蔚然成风。1984 年底，张君秋与费孝通、谢铁骊、浩然组成代表团出访日本，同中村歌右卫门等日本歌舞伎艺术家进行艺术交流，并亲切会见了日本的张派艺术爱好者。1990 年，应美华艺术协会的邀请出访美国，并接受美华艺术协会颁发的"终身艺术成就奖"及旧金山林肯大学颁发的"人文学"荣誉博士学位。他还应邀在哥伦比亚大学、圣地亚哥大学为学生讲学，并同华人广泛接触，宣传介绍京剧艺术。7 月回国后，受到李瑞环同志的亲切会见。为此，中国文联、中国戏剧家协会以及《中国戏剧》杂志社在人民大会堂召集首都文艺界人士座谈，热烈欢迎张君秋载誉归来。

　　In 1963, Zhang Jun-qiu and other performers put on plays in Hong Kong and enjoyed great popularity and success. Later on, his audiovisual products became more popular and spread even farther to the whole world. It became common practice for the funs in the United States and Japan to learn and perform the art of Zhang's school. At the end of 1984, Zhang Jun-qiu, together with Fei Xiao-tong, Xie Tie-li and Hao Ran, formed a visiting troupe to Japan. They made artistic exchanges with Japanese geishas like Nakamura and issued a meeting with the fans of the art of Zhang's school. In 1990, invited by Chinese American Art Association, he made a visit to America. He was awarded "Prize for Life-long Achievement in Art" by Chinese American Art Association and the "Honorary Humanity Doctorate" by Lincoln University. He was also invited to make speeches in Columbia University and Santiago University. He also made wide connection with American-born Chinese to spread the art of Peking Opera. After he came back to China in July he received warm welcome and interviewed by Li Rui-huan. National Literature and Art Association, Chinese Association of Drama and *Chinese Theatre* magazine held an informal discussion with the people from the cultural area in Beijing to celebrate the successful return of Zhang Jun-qiu.

与马连良、裘盛戎等到香港演出（1963）
Performing with Ma Lian-liang, Qiu Sheng-rong in Hong Kong (1963).

交游篇

艺播四海

①

②

奇双会
（写状起团圆止）

李奇，陕西褒城县人，贩马为业。妻王氏，生子保童，女桂枝，未几，王氏病死，继娶杨氏，性情乖张。趁李奇外出贩马，与地痞田旺私通，将保童与桂枝赶出门外。李奇回家询问子女下落，杨氏言语支吾。李奇拷打侍女春华，春华自缢身死。杨氏又与田旺串通，诬告李奇是奸，县官得贿，将李奇屈打成招，收入监中，等候处决（表演从这里开始）。新任褒城县令赵宠，偕夫人刘氏到任，(刘氏即桂枝，被河姓收留，嫁于赵宠。) 一日赵宠下乡劝农，桂枝闻内监内犯人啼哭甚惨，开监盘问，始知犯人即其亲父。等赵宠回衙，将其父冤情；向赵哭诉求救。赵宠设计代写状纸，令桂枝改扮做男装，到新任总抚衙行辕诉冤。那知总抚就是保童，当堂将其姊拉入后堂。赵宠见妻许久不出，奇身随进帐门，亦被保童拉入，经桂枝说明原委，共同商议为李奇申冤，于是一家骨肉复得团圆。

李桂枝……张君秋	赵　宠……姜妙香
李　奇……马盛龙	李保童……刘雪涛
胡老爷……李四广	

③

① 赴香港演出前，周恩来总理审查了赴港剧目，演出结束后接见张君秋等。左起：刘雪涛、言慧珠、张君秋、周恩来、姜妙香、俞振飞、马盛龙（1963）
Before leaving for Hong Kong, met by Premier Zhou En-lai. From left: Liu Xue-tao, Yan Hui-zhu, Zhang Jun-qiu, Zhou En-lai, Jiang Miao-xiang, Yu Zhen-fei, Ma Sheng-long (1963).

② ③ 周恩来保存的节目单
Performing list preserved by Zhou En-lai.

④ ⑤ 在香港演出《奇双会》。张君秋饰李桂枝，姜妙香饰赵宠（1963）
Performing *Selling Horse* in Hong Kong. Zhang Jun-qiu as Li Gui-zhi, Jiang Miao-xiang as Zhao Chong (1963).

① 在香港演出《奇双会》。张君秋饰李桂枝，刘雪涛饰李宝童（1963）
Performing *Selling Horse* in Hong Kong. Zhang Jun-qiu as Li Gui-zhi, Liu Xue-tao as Li Bao-Tong (1963).

② 在香港演出《望江亭》。张君秋饰谭记儿，刘雪涛饰白士中（1963）
Performing *Riverside Pavilion* in Hong Kong. Zhang Jun-qiu as Tan Ji-er, Liu Xue-tao as Bai Shi-zhong (1963).

交游篇

艺播四海

③

④

⑤

③ 在香港与孟小冬（左二）、马连良（1963）
With Meng Xiao-dong (second left), Ma Lian-liang(1963).

④ 在香港演出时与女儿学采合影，左为马连良
Photo taken with daughter Xue-cai while performing in Hong Kong, Ma Lian-liang (left).

⑤ 在香港演出《赵氏孤儿》，张君秋饰庄姬，马连良饰程婴，谭元寿饰孤儿（1963）
Performing Orphan of Zhao Family in Hong Kong. Zhang Jun-qiu as Concubine Zhuang, Ma Lian-liang as Cheng Ying, Tan Yuan-shou as Orphan (1963).

在香港演出《赵氏孤儿》后谢幕。左起：赵燕侠、何顺信、张君秋、马连良、薛恩厚、萨空了、姜妙香、肖甲、裘盛戎、马富禄、小王玉蓉（1963）

Answering the curtain call after performing *The Orphan of Zhao Family* in Hong Kong. From left: Zhao Yan-xia, He Shun-xin, Zhang Jun-qiu, Ma Lian-liang, Xue En-hou, Sa Kong-liao, Jiang Miao-xiang, Xiao Jia, Qiu Sheng-rong, Ma Fu-lu, junior Wang Yu-rong (1963).

① 荣获美国林肯大学颁发的人文学博士（1990.1）
Obtaining Humanity Doctorate from Lincoln University in January 1990.

② 荣获美国华美协会艺术中心颁发的"终身艺术成就奖"（1990.1）
Endowed with the prize for Life-long Achievement in Art from the Art Center of Sino-US Association of America in January 1990.

①

②

③

④

⑤

⑥

① 在哥伦比亚大学讲课
Lecturing in Colombia University.

② 在圣地亚哥大学讲学后与师生合影
Photo taken with the teachers and students of San Diego University.

③ 在华盛顿与美籍华人陈香梅（右二）会见
With American–born Chinese Chen Xiang-mei in Washington.

④ 与美国华人弟子任月娥、钟维娜、曹复莲、刘瑛
With his American Chinese prentices: Ren Yue-e, Zhong Wei-na, Cao Fu-lian, Liu Ying.

⑤ 同美国朋友
With American friends.

⑥ 同台湾弟子李忆萍
With Taiwanese prentice Li Yi-ping.

交游篇

艺播四海

①

②

③

④

⑤

① 与台湾京剧名家顾正秋相会在纽约
With Taiwanese well-known Peking Opera artist Gu Zheng-qiu in New York.

② 与台湾京剧演员徐露
With Taiwanese Peking Opera performer Xu Lu.

③ 在联合国会议室
In the conference hall of the United Nations Headquarters.

④ 在纽约联合国大厦门前
In front of the United Nations Headquarters, New York.

⑤ 在美国自由女神像前
In fromnt of the Statue of Liberty.

①

②

③

④

⑤

① 在好莱坞明星手足印迹前
At the fingerprints of Hollywood stars.

② 在夏威夷
In Hawaii.

③ 在拉斯维加斯
In Las Vegas.

④ 与费孝通（左一）、谢铁骊（右一）访问日本（1984）
Visiting Japan with Professor Fei Xiao-tong (first left), and film director Xie Tie-li(first right) (1984).

⑤ 会见日本歌舞伎艺术家尾上梅幸（1985）
Meeting Japanese geisha arist Omeka Oue(1985).

交游篇

艺播四海

①

②

① 会见日本歌舞伎艺术家中村歌佑卫门（1985）
Meeting Japanese geisha artist Nakamura(1985).

② 中村歌佑卫门演出后，张君秋表示祝贺，左一为浩然
Expressing congratulation to Nakamuras after the performance. Hao Ran (first left).

③ 在日本同张派艺术爱好者
With Japanese fans of Zhang's School.

④ 在日本公园游览
Touring in a park in Japan.

博识多才 Being of Great Learning and Great Ability

张君秋少年拜师学艺之后，因为学艺来之不易，在母亲的严格要求下，一天到晚都在紧张地练功、学戏、吊嗓、排戏。据他自己回忆，那时他唯一的业余爱好就是拍拍皮球。搭班演戏之后，除了学戏唱戏，他的业余生活增加了一个新的内容，就是绘画。他最早绘画的题材是兰花。那是他初露头角在上海歇夏时，向京剧老生演员时慧宝学来的。不足半月的时间，师徒所画的兰花真假难辨。当时，他不满20岁。随着张君秋艺业的精进，绘画的兴趣有增无减，不少书画大师如张大千、齐白石、刘海粟、黄胄、许麟庐都同他成了密友。他绘画的题材也日益增多，菊花、牡丹、水仙、荔枝、老来红、鱼、虾、鸡、竹，不下十余种。同他在戏曲艺术上追求创新一样，在绘画上也另辟蹊径。张君秋在绘画上自诩为"张大胆"。其实，他的艺术创作何尝不是"张大胆"呢？他的大胆是有着深厚的传统功底的。张君秋具有优异的音乐天赋，小时候，一把京胡拿在手中，几天的功夫，居然拉出了腔调。后来，他能拉得一手好京胡，这对于他以后创腔大有裨益。为了广征博采，收音机、录音机是他的好朋友。有时他晚上演戏，而另外一个剧场演着一个他想看的节目，他便委托朋友帮他去录音。完成演出任务之后，他再拿录音机"补课"。

Zhang Jun-qiu apprenticed himself to masters of Peking Opera when he was young. Because of the difficulty and the strict requirement of his mother, Zhang spent all of his childhood practicing, learning, training his voice and rehearsing. He recalled that bouncing balls was his only entertainment at that time. After becoming a member of the theatre troupe, besides learning and practicing, painting took a position in his life. Orchid was his first painting object. When he took his summer vacation in Shanghai, he learned to draw orchid from Shi Hui-bao, a personated old male role in Peking Opera. Less than half a month, when he was no more than 20, he caught up with his teacher in the proficiency of drawing orchid. With the rapid development of his painting skill, Zhang grew more interested in painting and became close friends with many experts of painting, such as Zhang Da-qian, Qi Bai-shi, Liu Hai-su, Huang Zhou and Xu Lin-lu. The objects of his painting increased to a dozen, namely the chrysanthemum, the peony, the narcissus, the litchi, the fish, the shrimp, the cock, the bamboo. Similar to his innovation of Peking Opera, Zhang also made innovation on painting. He cracked himself to be "audacious Zhang". In fact, the same was also true with his innovation on art. His audacity was deeply rooted in his solid basic skills. Actually, Zhang was gifted in music. With a "Jinghu" in hand, he can play the tune only several days later. Later, he became a master in playing "Jinghu", which did good to his future innovation on the tune of Peking Opera. In order to collect information, radio and tape recorder became his best friends. Sometimes he had a play to perform at night and at the same time another play appealing to him was on in another theatre. Therefore, he might ask one of his friends to record the play for him. He would listen to and learn it after his own performance.

作画
Drawing pictures.

同著名画家李苦禅
With the famous artist Li Ku-chan.

① 同著名画家刘海粟夫妇、黄胄夫妇合影
Photo taken with famous painter couples Liu Hai-su and Huang Zhou.

② 观刘海粟作画
Looking at Liu Hai-su drawing pictures.

同著名画家吴作人（中）、袁进修在一起
Together with famous painters Wu Zuo-ren(middle) and Yuan Jin-xiu.

①

②

③

④

① 与黄胄合作
Drawing pictures with famous painter Huang Zhou.

② 观赏黄胄作画
Looking at Huang Zhou drawing pictures.

③ 与著名画家周怀民、田世光合作
Drawing pictures with Zhou Huai-min, Tian Shi-guang.

④ 与著名画家徐北汀合作
Drawing pictures with famous painter Xu Bei-ding.

①

②

③

④

① 与著名画家许麟庐
With the famous artist Xu Lin-lu.

② 与著名画家陈大章合作
Drawing pictures with famous painter Chen Da-zhang.

③ 在全国政协书画联谊会上作画
Drawing pictures in the get-together of calligraphy and picture of CPPCC (Chinese People's Political Consultative Conference).

④ 为观众题写扇面
Writing calligraphy on the fan of an audience.

①

②

③

④ 张君秋七十寿辰，与夫人谢虹雯合影
Photo taken with his wife Xie Hong-wen on his 70th birthday.

⑤ 为谢虹雯题字
Inscribing for his wife Xie Hong-wen.

① 画前准备
Preparation before drawing.

② 准备作画
A bout to draw.

③ 作画
Drawing pictures.

张君秋书画作品　Zhang Jun-qiu's Calligraphy Works.

张君秋64寿辰时与李万春、荀令文、刘雪涛、吴素秋、许麟庐合作"花常好，人长寿，竹报平安"图

Drawing the picture named "flowers in full blossom, people in longevity and safety" with Li Wan-chun, Xun Ling-wen, Liu Xue-tao, Wu Su-qiu and Xu Lin-lu when he was 64 years old.

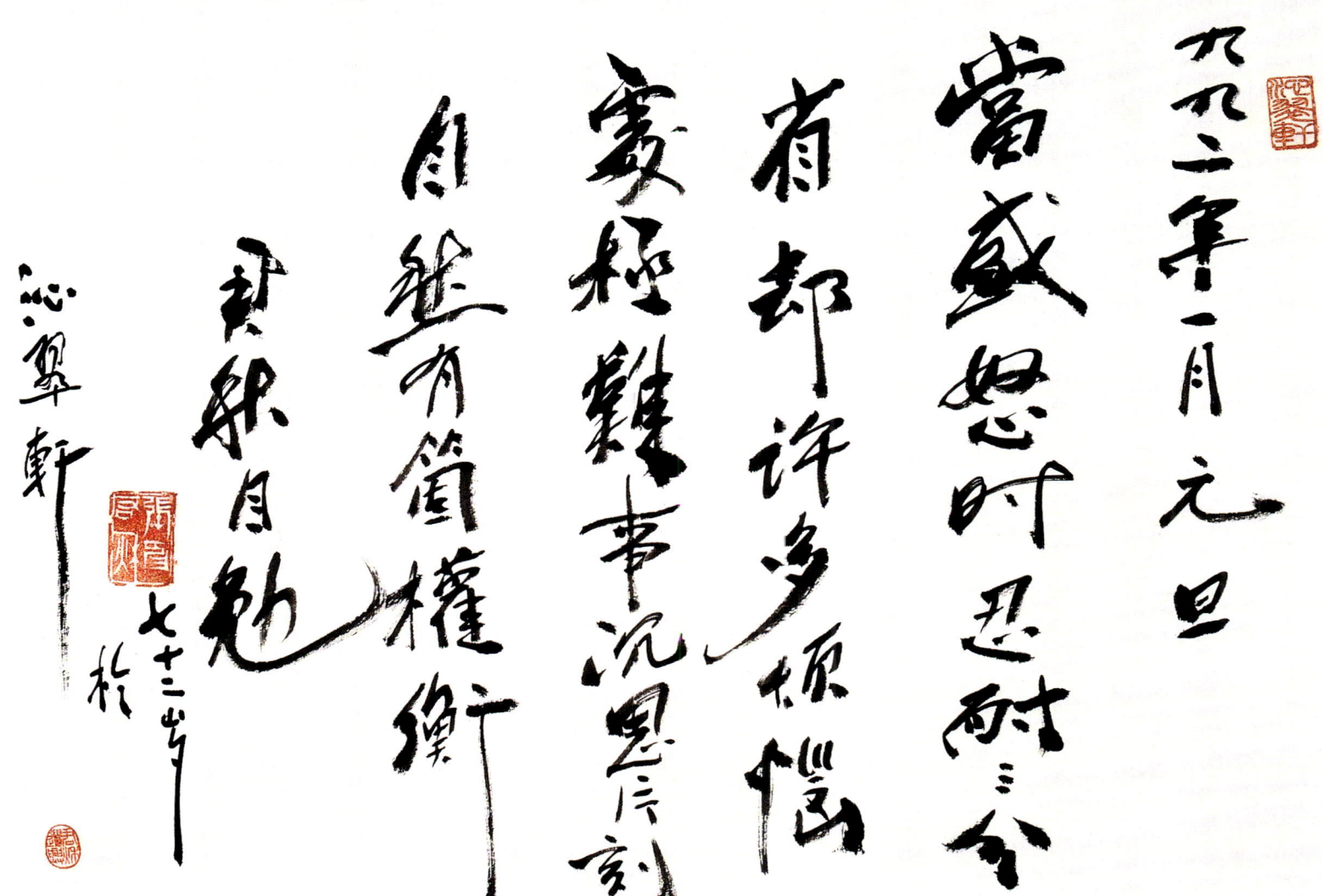

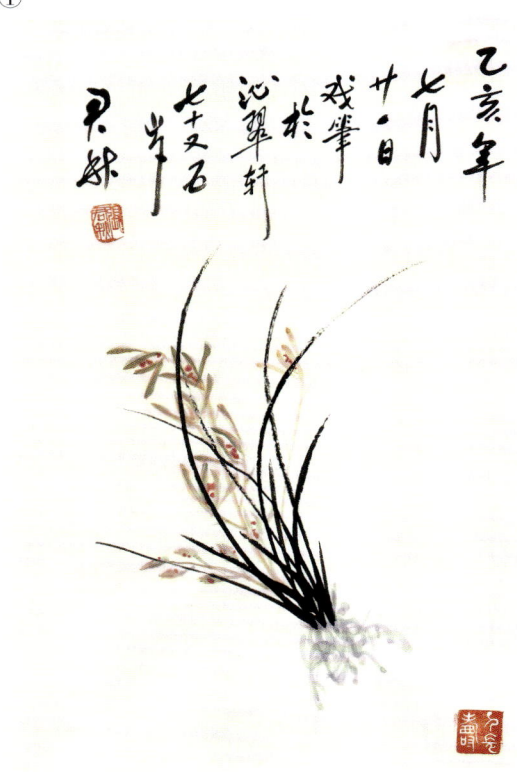

① 张君秋72岁时自勉题字："当盛怒时忍耐三分，省却许多烦恼；处极难事沉思片刻，自然有个权衡。"
Inscribing words to encourage himself when he was 72 years old: to endure patiently when irritated will save you many worries; to ponder carefully when troubled will offer you satisfactory answers.

② 75岁画兰花
Drawing orchids when he was 75.

③ "满园秋色"图
Picture named "Garden of Fall Scenery".

⑤

⑦

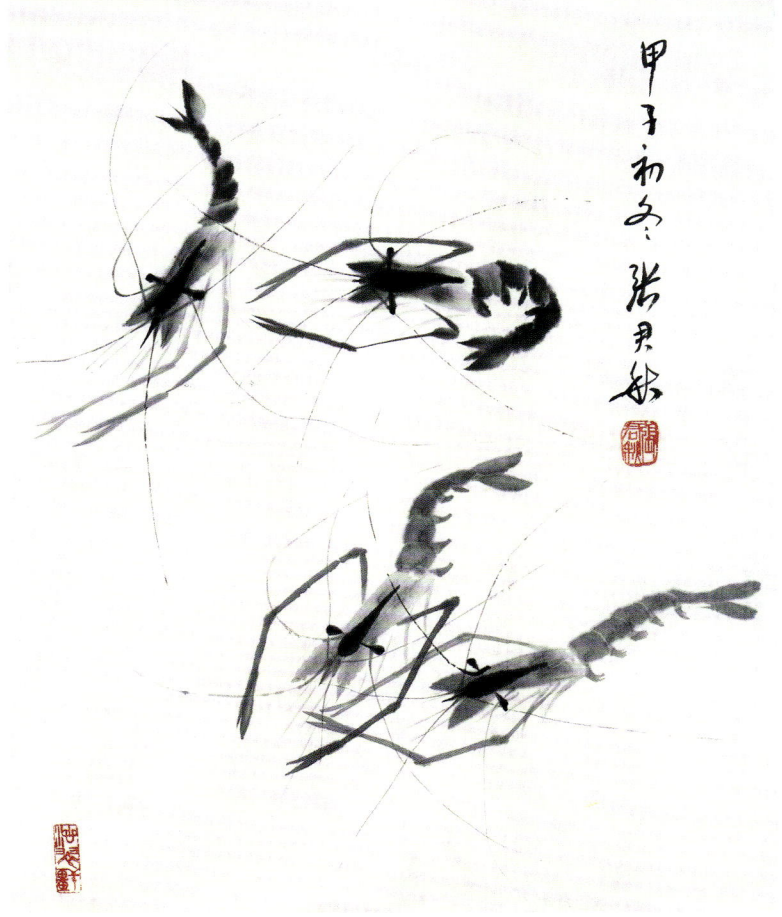

⑥

① 张君秋画鱼，娄师白补画荷花并题字
Zhang drew fish and Lou Shi-bai modified it with lotus and inscription.

② 吉利图
Picture named "Fortunate".

③ 张君秋、李万春、刘雪涛、吴素秋合作"富贵老来红"图
Picture named " the riches become popular when aged" drawn by Zhang Jun-qiu, Li Wan-chun, Liu Xue-tao, Wu Su-qiu.

④ 为京剧旦角邮折作
Drawing pictures for Dan (female role) in Peking Opera.

⑤ 75岁画萝卜白菜
Drawing carrot and cabbage when he was 75.

⑥ 虾
Shrimps.

⑦ 鱼乐图
Picture named "lively fish".

寿 Longevity

① 寿桃
Longevity Peach.

② 老来红、菊花
Chrysanthemum.

③ 鹰
Eagle.

④ 枇杷图
Loquat.

良师益友　Mentors

"转益多师"和"博采众长"是张君秋在艺业上取得成就的重要前提。张君秋不仅在京剧界转益多师，在影视界、话剧界、歌剧界、曲艺界，张君秋同样广交朋友，从他们那里，也得到了许多艺术营养，丰富了自己的艺术。张君秋在他的《谈戏曲青年演员的学习》一文中谈到博与精的关系，他说："艺术上的精是怎样来的呢？精是在博的基础上发展而成的。"要使自己的艺术达到精的程度，必须要摆好博与精的关系。他主张戏路要宽，学流派要广，行当要通，艺术要博，"不仅要精通戏曲表演，还要广泛学习、吸收其他艺术种类的营养，来丰富自己的表演。例如绘画、音乐、诗歌、文学、曲艺等，这些都是戏曲艺术创作不可缺少的艺术营养。"这是他的经验之谈。

"Learning from many experts" and "widely collecting others' advantages" are the basis of Zhang's great achievements in his career. He learnt not only from the experts in the field of Peking Opera but also from those in the field of film and television, modern drama, opera and acrobatics. He learnt a lot and benefited a lot from all of them. Zhang talked about the relations between being profound and being broad in his article "On the Learning of Young Peking Opera Performers". He said, "How does profoundness come into being? It has developed from broadness." The profoundness of one's art required the balance between being profound and being broad. He maintained various types of characters, broad grasp of different schools and in different roles, as well as a broad understanding of art. He also said, according to his experience, "A Peking Opera performer should not only be a master of performing but should also widely learn and assimilate advantages of others in order to perfect oneself. Drawing, music, poetry, literature and acrobatics are all indispensable to the perfection of one's own art."

① 同刘雪涛（左一）、何顺信（左二）、张似云（右一）
With Liu Xue-tao(first left), He Shun-xin (second left), Zhang Si-yun(first right).

①

②

③

① 同京剧名家梅葆玖（右）、梅葆玥交谈
Talking with famous Peking Opera artists Mei Bao-jiu (right), Mei Bao-yue.

② 与梅派弟子。沈小梅（前排中）、李玉芙（前右一）、陈伯华（后左三）、李玉茹（后左四）、梅葆玖（后左六）、梅葆玥（后右一）、杨荣环（后右四）、高玉倩（后右五）
With the prentices of Mei's School, Shen Xiao-mei (middle in the front row), Li Yu-fu (front row, first right), Cheng Bo-hua (back row, third left), Li Yu-ru (back row, fourth left), Mei Bao-jiu (back row, sixth left), Mei Bao-yue (back row, first right), Yang Rong-huan (back row, fourth right), Gao Yu-qian (back row, fifth right).

③ 同著名戏剧家黄宗江（左二）、刘曾复（右三）、刘雪涛（右二）以及梅兰芳之子梅绍武（右一）
With famous playwright Huang Zong-jiang (second), Liu Zeng-fu (third right), Liu Xue-tao (second right) and Mei Shao-wu, son of Mei Lan-fang (first right).

① 同天津市中华民族文化促进会会长方放
With head of Tianjin Chinese National Culture Promotion Association Mr. Fang Fang.

② 同香港名票包幼蝶
With Hong Kong amateur performer Bao You-die.

与俞振飞切磋《奇双会》(1989)
Discussing with Yu Zhen-fei on *Selling Horse* (1989).

交游篇

良师益友

①

②

③

④

⑤

⑥

⑦

① ② 《奇双会》中饰李桂枝，俞振飞饰赵宠（1981）
In *Selling Horse* as Li Gui-zhi, Yu Zhen-fei as Zhao Chong(1981).

③ 李丽华看张君秋化妆
Li Li-hua looking at Zhang Jun-qiu when he put on make-up.

④ 同俞振飞合作《春秋配》后，香港影星李丽华上台献花祝贺。右三为童芷苓（1981）
Hong Kong film star Li Li-hua expressed congratulations to him after his cooperation with Yu Zhen-fei in *The Match of Spring and Autumn*. Tong Zhi-ling (third right)(1981).

⑤ 同京剧名家白登云
With famous Peking Opera artist Bai Deng-yun.

⑥ 同京剧名家高盛麟
With famous Peking Opera artist Gao Sheng-lin.

⑦ 同京剧名家吴素秋（中）、李砚秀
With famous Peking Opera artist Wu Su-qiu (middle), Li Yan-qiu.

① 同京剧名家李玉茹（前右一）、上海市文化局局长马博敏（后右）、上海京剧院院长黎中城（后左）
With famous Peking Opera artist Li Yu-ru (front row, first right), Ma Bo-min (back row, right), Director of Shanghai Culture Bureau, Li Zhong-cheng (back row, left), Chairman of Shanghai Peking Opera Theatre.

② 同京剧名家李万春（左）、相声名家侯宝林
With famous Peking Opera artist Li Wan-chun (left), cross-talk master Hou Bao-lin.

③ 同京剧名家杨荣环
With famous Peking Opera artist Yang Rong-huan.

① 同京剧名家关肃霜等在一起。前排左起：张继青、李炳淑、李维康、王兴华；后排：杜家福、刘开宇、方荣翔、梅葆玖、张君秋、关肃霜、叶少兰、张卉、贾志刚、卢子明
With famous Peking Opera artist Guan Su-shuang and others. Front row: Zhang Ji-qing, Li Bing-shu, Li Wei-kang, Wang Xing-hua; back row: Du Jia-fu, Liu Kai-yu, Fang Rong-xiang, Mei Bao-jiu, Zhang Jun-qiu, Guan Su-shuang, Ye Shao-lan, Zhang Hui, Jia Zhi-gang, Lu Zi-ming.

② 同京剧名家刘秀荣、张春孝夫妇
With famous Peking Opera artist Liu Xiu-rong and her husband Zhang Chun-xiao.

交游篇

良师益友

① 同京剧名家刘长瑜（右）、宋玉珍
With famous Peking Opera artist Liu Chang-yu (right), Song Yu-zhen.

② 同京剧名家李维康
With famous Peking Opera artist Li Wei-kang.

③ 同著名学者冯牧（左一）、美国京剧名票谢国振（左三）、梅兰芳儿媳屠珍（右三）、京剧名家孙毓敏（右一）
With famous scholar Feng Mu (first left), American amateur performer Xie Guo-zhen (third left), Mei Lan-fang's daughter-in-law Tu Zhen (third right), famous Peking Opera artist Sun Yu-min (first right).

④ 同豫剧表演艺术家常香玉及著名戏剧家赵寻、刘厚生等。左起，前排：谢虹雯、兰光、常香玉、傅惠珍；后排：段大雄、张君秋、陈宪章、赵寻、刘厚生、安志强
With Henan Opera performing artist Chang Xiang-yu and well-known playwright Zhao Xun, Liu Hou-sheng. From left, front row: Xie Hong-wen, Lan Guang, Chang Xiang-yu, Fu Hui-zhen; back row: Duan Da-xiong, Zhang Jun-qiu, Cheng Xian-zhang, Zhao Xun, Liu Hou-sheng, An Zhi-qiang.

交游篇

良师益友

①

②

③

④

⑤

⑥

① 同粤剧名家红线女
With famous Guangdong Opera artist Hong Xian-nv.

② 同香港影星夏梦（右一）、京剧名家宋丹菊
With Hong Kong film star Xia Meng (first right), famous Peking Opera artist Song Dan-ju.

③ 同晋剧名家贾桂林（右一）、狮子黑（左一）
With famous Shanxi Opera artis: Jia Gui-lin (first right), Shi Zi-hei (first left).

④ 同曲艺名家骆玉笙
With famous folk performing artist Luo Yu-sheng.

⑤ 同著名歌唱家郭兰英
With famous singer Guo Lan-yirg.

⑥ 同著名电影演员古月
With famous film actor Gu Yue.

①

②

③

④

⑤

⑥

① 同法国著名服装设计师皮尔卡丹
With famous French fashion designer Pierre Cardin.

② 同香港著名报人沈苇窗
With Shen Wei-chuang, famous Hong Kong newspaperman.

③ 同著名话剧演员蓝天野（右）、刘雪涛
With famous drama actor Lan Tian-ye (right), Liu Xue-tao.

④ 同香港京剧名票李和声、李尤婉云夫妇
With famous Hong Kong amateur performer Li He-sheng and his wife Li You-wan.

⑤ 同香港京剧名票金如新（左）、李和声（右）
With famous Hong Kong amateur performers Jin Ru-xin (left), Li He-sheng (right).

⑥ 同台湾企业家吴昌涛
With Taiwan entrepreneur Wu Chang-tao.

① 同粤剧著名演员新马师曾夫妇
With famous Guangdong opera performer: Xin Ma Shi-zeng and his wife.

② 同香港京剧名票钱江夫妇
With famous Hong Kong amateur performer Qian Jiang and his wife.

③ 同香港京剧名票金如新（右二）、张雨文（左二），天津立达集团董事长葛子平（右一）
With famous Hong Kong amateur performer Jin Ru-xin(secomd right), Zhang Yu-wen(second left), Tianjin Li Da Group, head of the board,Ge Zi-ping (first right).

北京国际票房成立时的合影。左起前排：林瑞康、耿其昌、梅葆玥、韩力、顾恺章、李世济、高占祥、张君秋、梅葆玖、张百发、钱江、叶少兰、黄定、杨洁、刘雪涛；中排：谢国祥、谢虹雯、李维康、许嘉宝、张学津；三排：唐在忻、沈绮琅

Photo taken when Beijing International Box Office was set up. Front row, from left: Lin Rui-kang, Geng Qi-chang, Mei Bao-yue, Han Li, Gu Kai-zhang, Li Shi-ji, Gao Zhan-xiang, Zhang Jun-qiu, Mei Bao-jiu, Zhang Bai-fa, Qian Jiang, Ye Shao-lan, Huang Ding, Yang Jie, Liu Xue-tao; second row: Xie Guo-xiang, Xie Hong-wen, Li Wei-kang, Xu Jia-bao, Zhang Xue-jin ; third row: Tang Zai-xin, Shen Qi-lang.

闲情逸趣　Leisurely and Carefree Mood

旅游是张君秋业余生活的最爱。大江南北，山川河海，都是他陶冶性情的所在。这些，也都离不开他对戏曲创作的思考，看到了楼台亭阁，有时就引起了他对《望江亭》中亭子布景的设想。走进晋祠，看到了宋代的仕女泥塑，不由得仔细端详，把这些同京剧舞台上的扮相服装联系起来。他又是一个美食家。不是因为他在饮食上多么挑剔，重要的是吃要吃出情趣，煮饺子他要几个几个地煮，不要叫它凉了而要热乎乎地吃下，别有"韵味"。吃面条愿意吃抻面，因为它筋道有劲。戏班里有句话，叫做"饱吹饿唱"，张君秋反其道而行之，唱戏前决不饿着，而是要吃饱吃好。他的理论是，嗓子是身体的一部分，身体好了，嗓子自然就好。美食家同艺术家是紧密相连的。

　　Traveling was his favorite entertainment. He aimed to travel across every scenic spot in the world. This was also connected with his innovation of Peking Opera. The scene of attics and pavilions always brought him to mind the arrangement of the pavilion in *Riverside Pavilion*. Walking into the Jin Memorial Hall and seeing the clothes of the Maids, Zhang carefully observed them and related these to the clothing ornament on the stage. Zhang was also a belly-God. He was not critical about food. He just wanted to have some fun. Whining boiling dumplings, he wanted them boiled in twos and threes and took them before they turned cool. He considered it "lingering charm". He liked hand-pulled noodles, for they are more elastic. There prevailed a saying in the theatre troupe, "full blows hungrily sings". But he acted in a diametrically opposite way. He must have a good dinner before performing. He maintained that throat is an integral part of the body and a beautiful voice depended on a healthy body. A belly-God was in consistency with an artist.

爬山
Climbing.

① 与女儿张学敏在家中留影
Photo taken with daughter Zhang Xue-min at home.

② 辅导张学聪排练节目。左，张学津；右，张学玲
Helping Zhang Xue-cong rehearse. Left: Zhang Xue-jin; right: Zhang Xue-ling.

交游篇

闲情逸趣

①

②

③

④

⑤

⑥

① 张君秋之外孙女中国京剧院演员王润菁
Zhang Jun-qiu's granddaughter Wang Run-qing, a performer from Academy of Chinese Traditional Peking Opera.

② 指导长子张学津学习书法
Teaching eldest son Zhang Xue-jin to learn calligraphy.

③ 辅导外孙女卢思排练《贵妃醉酒》
Helping granddaughter Lu Si play *Drunken Concubine*.

④ 教张学沄拉京胡
Teaching Zhang Xue-yun to play the Jinghu (a two-stringed bowed instrument with a high register).

⑤ 人高"马"大
Sitting high on a big "horse".

⑥ 在陶然亭放风筝
Fly kite besides Tao Ran Pavilion.

交游篇

闲情逸趣

①

②

交游篇

闲情逸趣

③

④

⑤

① ② 在晋祠仕女旁流连忘返
Deeply attracted by the gorgeous servant girl in Jin temple.

③ 喜爱兰花
Affection for orchid.

④ 赏花
Appreciating flowers.

⑤ 雪后登长城
Climbing the Great Wall after snow.

交游篇 闲情逸趣

②

①

③

④

① 在香港大佛前（1996）
In front of Buddhist figure, Hong Kong (1996).

② 游览山东蓬莱阁
Visiting Penglai Attic.

③ 在甘露寺前品味《甘露寺》
Savouring *Sweet Dew Temple* before Sweet Dew Temple.

④ 在北戴河海滨
At the seaside of Beidaihe City.

①

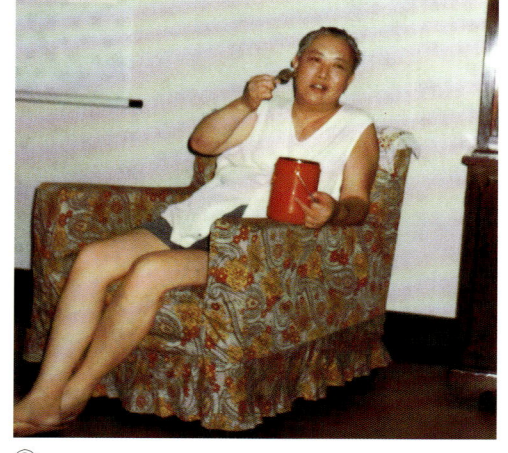
③

②

1997年5月27日，张君秋在去"音配像"现场途中因心脏病复发，
抢救无效，不幸逝世。
6月16日，乔石、李瑞环等中央领导同志及首都各界人士
在北京八宝山公墓向张君秋作最后告别。
张君秋的去世引起人们对他的深切缅怀，
他创造的张派艺术流传海内外，是中国戏曲艺术宝库中的珍贵财富。
他对京剧事业的一片挚爱和热诚深深打动着我们，
特别是在他晚年致力于《中国京剧音配像精粹》
工程的敬业献身精神更值得我们深切怀念。
张君秋和他创立的张派艺术是人们心中不朽的丰碑。

On May 27th, 1997, on his way to the spot of audio-videotaping works, Zhang Jun-qiu died of heart attack. On June 16th, national leaders Qiao Shi, Li Rui-huan and people from all walks of life bid farewell to Zhang Jun-qiu at Beijing Babaoshan public cemetery. Zhang's departure caused people to cherish the memory of him. Zhang's School spread all over the world and was the valuable treasure of traditional Chinese drama treasury. His love and sincerity to Peking Opera deeply moved us. People were especially moved by his wholehearted devotion to "Peking Opera Audio-video taped Classics".
Immortality to Zhang Jun-qiu and Zhang's School!

IMMORTALITY 流芳篇

身后哀荣 Posthumous Fame　　**音容宛在** Being Remembered Forever

身后哀荣

中国共产党优秀党员、我国著名京剧艺术大师、戏曲教育家、政协第八届全国委员会常委、政协全国委员会科教文卫体委员会副主任、中国文学艺术界联合会副主席、中国戏曲学院顾问张君秋同志,因病抢救无效,于1997年5月27日12时20分在北京逝世,享年77岁。

6月16日,北京八宝山公墓礼堂哀乐低回,首都各界人士冒着酷暑来到这里,为张君秋送行。

乔石、李瑞环、丁关根、李铁映、王兆国、万国权,以及中央国家机关有关部门的负责同志,艺术界张君秋的同行朋友、弟子们默默来到灵前,向大师作最后的告别。

张君秋安卧在鲜花丛中,一只只盛满哀思的花圈环绕四周。江泽民、李鹏、乔石、李瑞环、朱镕基、刘华清、胡锦涛、荣毅仁、丁关根、田纪云、李岚清、李铁映、邹家华、姜春云、尉健行、万里、宋平、薄一波、宋任穷、雷洁琼、王光英、叶选平、王兆国、杨静仁、钱伟长、万国权、何鲁丽等领导同志和习仲勋、彭冲、郑天翔、刘复之等老同志,以及中央和国家机关的负责同志,或送来花圈表示哀悼,或以不同方式向张君秋的亲属表示慰问。中组部、中宣部、中央统战部、全国政协办公厅、文化部、中国文联等单位也送来花圈。5月27日张君秋逝世的当天,正在国外访问的李瑞环同志亲自打回电话向张君秋家属表示慰问和哀悼,回国后又专程到其家中吊唁。

八宝山公墓灵堂
Condolence hall of Babaoshan Cemetery.

Posthumous Fame

Excellent party member of CPC, well-known Peking Opera master, educator of drama, the standing committee member of the 8th political consulting committee, deputy director of the committee of Science, Education, Arts, Public Health and Sports, vice president of Chinese Art and Literature League, counselor of Chinese Academy of Drama, Comrade. Zhang Jun-qiu passed away at 12:20, May 27th, 1997 at the age of 77.

On June 16th, the funeral music was filled in Beijing Babaoshan public cemetery. People from all walks of life in Beijing came under heat to bid farewell to Zhang Jun-qiu.

Qiao Shi, Li Rui-huan, Ding Guan-gen, Li Tie-ying, Wang Zhao-guo, Wan Guo-quan and other leaders in charge of relevant departments, friends and prentices of Zhang Jun-qiu came in silence to the front of the coffin and bid farewell to the Master.

Zhang lied in the middle of fresh flowers and wreaths filled with sorrow surrounded the hall. National leaders Jiang Ze-min, Li Peng, Qiao Shi, Li Rui-huan, Zhu Rong-ji, Liu Hua-qing, Hu Jin-tao, Rong Yi-ren, Ding Guan-gen, Tian Ji-yun, Li Lan-qing, Li Tie-ying, Zou Jia-hua, Jiang Chun-yun, Wei Jian-xing, Wan Li, Song Ping, Bo Yi-bo, Song Ren-qiong, Lei Jie-qiong, Wang Guang-ying, Ye Xuan-ping, Wang Zhao-guo, Yang Jing-ren, Qian Wei-chang, Wan Guo-quan, He Lu-li and aged comrades Xi Zhong-xun, Peng Chong, Zheng Tian-xiang, Liu Fu-zhi and other leaders in charge either came with wreaths or saluted to Zhang in various ways. Center group, Chinese Propaganda Department, Central United Front Activities Department, National Political Consultative Conference General Office, Ministry of Culture, National Literature and Art Association also sent wreaths to express sorrow. On May 27th, Li Rui-huan, who was on his way of visiting abroad telephoned to express his sorrow and mourns and made a special trip to his home after coming back.

党和国家领导人江泽民、李鹏、乔石、李瑞环、朱镕基、刘华清、胡锦涛送来花圈，对张君秋逝世表示哀悼

State leaders Jiang Ze-min, Li Peng, Qiao Shi, Li Rui-huan, Zhu Rong-ji, Liu Hua-qing, and Hu Jin-tao sent wreaths to express condolence.

① 李瑞环到张君秋家中吊唁，慰问家属
In Zhang Jun-qiu's home, Li Rui-huan expressing condolence to his grieved family members.

② 首都各界人士送别张君秋
People of different walks in Beijing saying farewell to his body.

流芳篇

身后哀荣

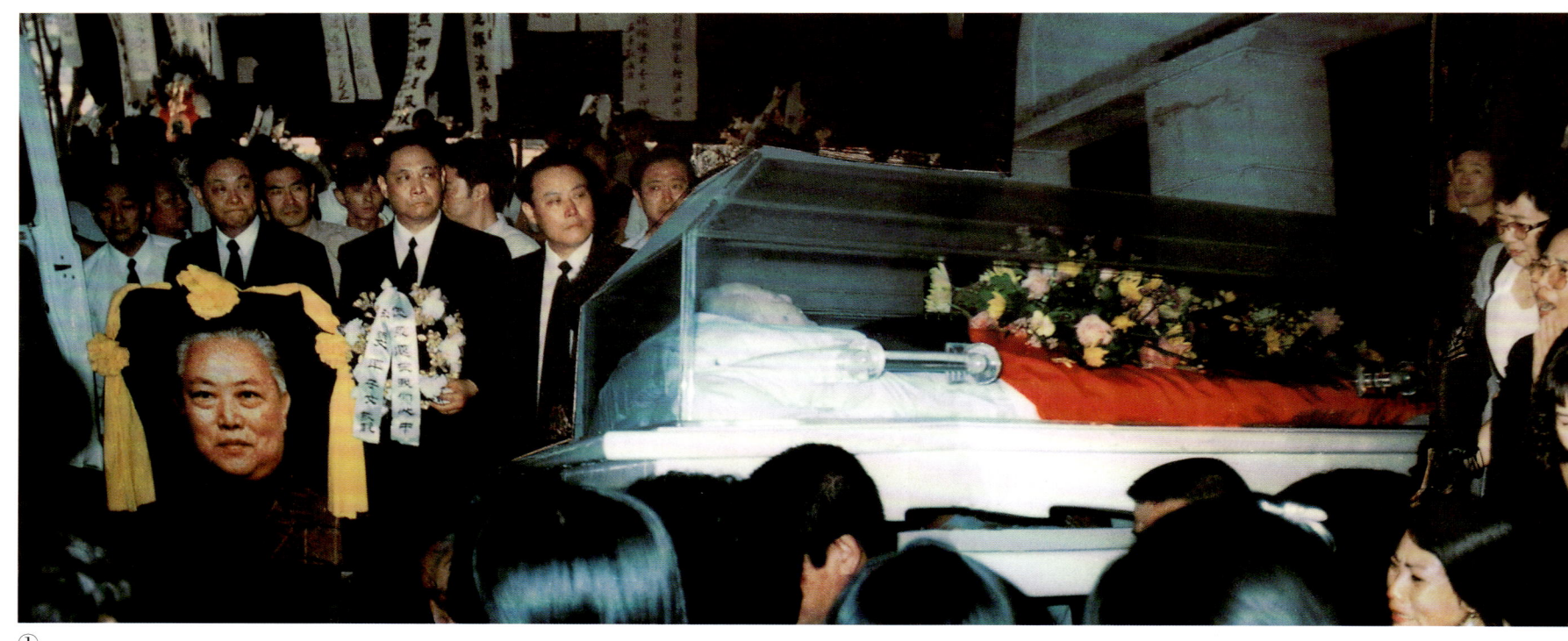

①

②

① 张君秋灵柩前
In front of Zhang's coffin.

② 部分报刊纪念张君秋文章
Some articles in memorial of Zhang Jun-qiu.

③《人民日报》报道首都各界人士送别张君秋
Reports of People's Daily about people of different walks in Beijing saying farewell to his body.

音容宛在 Being Remembered Forever

音容宛在

流芳篇

音容宛在

流芳篇 音容宛在

流芳篇

音容宛在

张君秋生平大事年表

Lifetime Events of Zhang Jun-qiu.

张君秋生平大事年表

1920年10月14日	（农历九月初三）生于北京。
	父滕联芳，职员。母，张秀琴，河北梆子青衣演员。幼从父姓，名滕家鸿。学艺后从母姓，名张君秋。
1926–1932年	上私塾、平民小学。
	随母到保定、张家口一带演出。
1933年	拜李凌枫学习京剧青衣艺术，以《彩楼配》、《女起解》、《二进宫》、《祭江》等戏开蒙。
	李凌枫的老师王瑶卿开始向其隔辈授艺。
1936年	春节前，在吉祥戏院首次登台，演出《女起解》。
	借台演戏，曾与李多奎同台演出《大登殿》，与谭小培、郝寿臣、慈瑞泉同台演出《法门寺》，与姜妙香同台演出《会审》。
	遇尚小云，得其赏识。入尚家请益，学《春秋配》、《御碑亭》等戏。随尚小云搭长庆社，与尚小云同台演出《乾坤福寿镜》、《九曲黄河阵》、《牛郎织女》等戏。
1937年	2–4月，搭王又宸班，首次去天津中国大戏院演出，剧目为《大保国、探皇灵、二进宫》、《四郎探母》等。

与孟小冬在天津演出，剧目为《四郎探母》、《御碑亭》。

5月，搭马连良"扶风社"，首次去上海演出，在黄金大戏院演出《龙凤呈祥》、《法门寺》、《苏武牧羊》、《四进士》、《清风亭》、《打渔杀家》、《审头刺汤》等。

在上海拜梅兰芳为师，学《凤还巢》、《生死恨》、《霸王别姬》、《宇宙锋》、《奇双会》等。

1938年	2月，搭王又宸班至天津演出。
	2月，搭马连良"扶风社"，在北平新新戏院演出。
	3月，搭谭富英"扶春社"，在天津中国大戏院演出。
	4月，搭谭富英"扶春社"，在北平华乐戏院演出。
	5月，随谭富英"扶春社"，至上海黄金大戏院演出。
	6-7月，在上海歇夏，向冯子和学花旦戏，向郑传鉴、朱传铭学昆曲。
	8月，搭马连良"扶风社"，在上海演出。
1938—1941年	以搭马连良"扶风社"为主，兼与金少山、谭富英等著名演员合作。
	继续在王瑶卿家学戏。
	《立言画刊》广泛征求读者意见，约请社会知名人士磋商，议定李世芳、毛世来、张君秋、宋德珠为"四小名旦"。
1940年	同赵玉蓉女士结婚。
1941年	向李凌枫学戏期满，脱离"扶风社"。
	程砚秋向其传授《朱痕记》、《红拂传》、《贺后骂殿》、《金锁记》等戏。
1942年	组"谦和社"，任主演，赵砚奎任社长。
	何顺信入"谦和社"。初，李德山京胡，何顺信二胡，后何顺信主操京胡。

"谦和社"主要阵容：老生贯盛习、张春彦、纪玉良，花脸侯喜瑞、刘连荣、袁世海、王泉奎，小生姜妙香、叶盛兰、尚富霞，武生孙毓堃、周瑞安，刀马旦阎世善、李金鸿，老旦李多奎，丑行萧长华、高富远、萧盛萱。

经常演出的剧目为《四郎探母》《红鬃烈马》《法门寺》《御碑亭》《玉堂春》《孙尚香》《骊珠恨》《困龙床》《金山寺、断桥、雷峰塔》《大保国、二进宫》《武昭关》《雁门关》《琵琶缘》《混元盒》《缇萦救父》《生死恨》《凤还巢》《霸王别姬》《宇宙锋》《奇双会》《汉明妃》《红拂传》《朱痕记》《金锁记》等。

1943年	父滕联芳去世。 9月，"谦和社"至天津演出，剧目为《玉堂春》《金山寺、断桥、雷峰塔》《王春娥》《四郎探母》等。 11月，"谦和社"去上海演出，剧目为《玉堂春》《霸王别姬》《凤还巢》《四郎探母》《汉明妃》《凤双栖》等。向顾正秋传授《汉明妃》。
1944年	同吴励箴女士结婚。 9月，"谦和社"解散。
1945—1947年	成立"秋社"，自任社长、主演。创演《怜香伴》《银屏公主》《奇烈记》等。
1948年	应孙兰亭之约，同马连良、俞振飞赴香港普庆戏院演出。
1949年	应香港胜利影片之约，同马连良拍戏曲影片《梅龙镇》《打渔杀家》，同俞振飞拍戏曲影片《玉堂春》。 留居香港，间有演出，与马连良、俞振飞、程正泰、汪正华等合作。
1951年	10月，由香港返回内地。
1951—1952年	在武汉参加中南联谊京剧团，同马连良、高盛麟、高维廉、郭元汾、叶盛茂、张金梁等合作。

1952年	随联谊京剧团至南昌演出，沿途北上，经天津，抵达北京。在北京受到周恩来总理的接见。周恩来勉励张君秋说："爱国不分早晚，革命不分先后。回来就好，希望你多做贡献。" 在北京组建北京联谊京剧团，年底改名为北京市京剧三团。主要成员有陈少霖、高维廉、冀韵兰、李四广、朱金琴、耿世华、郝庆海、钮荣亮等。
1953-1955年	创演《刘兰芝》、《彩楼记》。高维廉离去，刘雪涛加入。
1956年	参加慰问中国人民志愿军代表团，赴朝慰问演出。 创演《望江亭》，在上海首演。 北京市京剧三团同马连良京剧团、北京市京剧二团合并，组成北京京剧团。 北京京剧团的阵容： 主演，马连良、谭富英、张君秋、裘盛戎， 生行陈少霖、马盛龙、刘盛通、谭元寿、马长礼、高宝贤， 旦行李毓芳、李世济、小王玉蓉， 小生行刘雪涛、茹富华、闵兆华， 净行周和桐、张洪祥、马崇仁、郝庆海， 武生行杨盛春、黄元庆、杨少春， 老旦行李多奎、耿世华， 丑行马富禄、慈少泉、李四广、郭元祥、钮荣亮等。
1958年	创演《珍妃》。 拍摄戏曲影片《望江亭》。
1959年	创演《秋瑾》。 创演《秦香莲》（同马连良、谭富英、裘盛戎合作）。 创演《赵氏孤儿》（同马连良、谭富英、裘盛戎合作）。 创演《西厢记》（同中国京剧院叶盛兰、杜近芳合作）。
1960年	创演《状元媒》（同马连良、谭富英合作）。

生平大事年表

1961年	创演《楚宫恨》(同谭富英合作)。
1962年	率演出小组赴武汉参加武汉京剧团演出。 创演《诗文会》。
1963年	4月同马连良、裘盛戎率北京京剧团赴香港、澳门演出《赵氏孤儿》、《秦香莲》、《望江亭》、《状元媒》、《奇双会》等。赴港演出前，周恩来总理观看了《望江亭》演出，对该剧予以肯定和鼓励，并提出修改意见。年中，拍摄戏曲影片《秦香莲》。
1964年	参加《芦荡火种》导演团，并演出《芦荡火种》。 为北京市实验京剧团新剧目《海棠峪》设计唱腔。
1965年	调北京京剧二团。创演《年年有余》(同马连良合作)。
1966-1967年	"文革"开始，被迫停止演出。
1968年	母张秀琴去世。
1969年	夫人吴励箴去世。
1970-1973年	恢复工作，参加中国京剧院《红色娘子军》、《平原作战》、《红灯照》创作。
1974年	夫人赵玉蓉去世。 同谢虹雯女士结婚。
1978年	调回北京京剧院（原北京京剧团），恢复舞台生活。 夏，应史若虚邀请，同史带领中国戏曲学院实验京剧团赴烟台演出。张君秋恢复演出传统戏《苏三起解》。

秋，遵照周总理生前意见，着手《望江亭》剧本的修改整理，并在"卖鱼"一场增创新唱段。借中国戏曲学院排演场进行排演，并公演。

1979年

调中国戏曲学院任副院长。

夏，着手整理、修改《西厢记》，并恢复演出。

开始陆续在《人民日报》《北京日报》《北京晚报》《中国戏剧》（原《戏剧报》）、《艺术研究》等报刊发表艺术研究文章。

1980年

在北京、天津演出《西厢记》。

3月，陆续整理恢复《法门寺》、《苏三起解》等传统剧目的演出。

1981年

5月，赴上海参加俞振飞舞台生活60年庆祝活动，并与俞振飞同台演出《奇双会》、《春秋配》。

6月，加入中国共产党。

7月，指导中国戏曲学院学生排演传统剧目《四郎探母》，由张君秋的学生王蓉蓉、张静琳、徐美玲等主演的《四郎探母》在北京天桥剧场连续演出10场。

11月，在北京工人俱乐部恢复演出经整理加工的传统剧目《银屏公主》。

1982年

与刘雪涛、郭元祥、钮荣亮、耿世华、何顺信、张似云等对中国戏曲学院即将毕业的大学本科生王蓉蓉、张静琳、宋小川、吕昆山等实行"一对一"教学辅导，排演《望江亭》。该剧在北京、上海等地作汇报演出，很受欢迎。

夏，与高盛麟、李盛藻等在中国戏曲学院排演场为学生示范演出《龙凤呈祥》。

1983年

6月，时任天津市市长李瑞环同志为团长，张君秋为副团长组成慰问团，至引滦入津工程慰问演出。

1984年

10月1日，登天安门城楼，参加国庆35周年观礼。

	11月，在中央电视台录制戏曲电视片《诗文会》。
	12月，任赴日代表团副团长出访日本。
1985年	6-8月，赴香港中文大学讲学。
	恢复演出《状元媒》。
1986年	天津日报社举办庆祝张君秋舞台生活50周年演出。李瑞环观看了演出活动。张君秋的弟子薛亚萍、王婉华、杨淑蕊、关静兰、张学敏、刘明珠、王蓉蓉、张静琳、徐美玲、张晓虹、孙爱珍，张君秋的子女张学津、张学玲、张学华、张学聪等参加了演出。
	应李瑞环的邀请，张君秋担任天津市青年京剧团"百日集训"艺术总顾问。
1987年	作为艺术总顾问，率天津市青年京剧团赴香港演出。
1989年	获金唱片奖。
	10月，赴上海，参加上海电视台主办的庆贺"星期戏曲广播会"双百华诞活动，同俞振飞清唱《奇双会》。
	12月底，应美国美华艺术协会邀请，赴美访问。
1990年	接受美华协会颁发的"终身艺术成就奖"及旧金山林肯大学颁发的"人文学荣誉博士"学位。
	7月，回国。
	7月12日，首都文艺界、戏剧界在人民大会堂安徽厅举行欢迎张君秋载誉归来座谈会。
	12月，在纪念徽班晋京200年开幕式上演出《龙凤呈祥》。
1991年	1月，赴福建参加福建电视台新年晚会。

	10月，赴天津出席天津市文化局主办的祝贺'91和平杯中国京剧票友邀请赛张派艺术演唱会。
1992年	夏，再次赴美。心脏病发作。
1993年	首都戏剧界、文艺界举行庆祝张君秋艺术生活60周年活动。中共中央政治局常委乔石、李瑞环出席了庆祝活动开幕式。文化部常务副部长高占祥代表文化部致开幕词，中国文联主席、中国剧协主席曹禺发来贺信，文化部部长刘忠德为张君秋颁发了题有"艺高德劭，继往开来"的表彰状。庆祝活动期间，张君秋弟子薛亚萍、杨淑蕊、关静兰、王蓉蓉、董翠娜、张萍、赵秀君等参加了演出。张君秋子女张学津、张学海、张学济、张学浩、张学敏、张学华、张学玲、张学治、张学江、张学泛等满堂儿孙联袂演出《龙凤呈祥》。海外华人也参加了演出。
1994年	应李瑞环邀请，张君秋担任《中国京剧音配像精粹》艺术总顾问。
1995年	心脏病二次发作。经复外医院抢救，病情平稳后，继续从事京剧音配像工作。 11月，作为嘉宾参加在天津举办的首届中国京剧艺术节。
1996年	从事京剧音配像工作。
1997年	从事京剧音配像工作。 5月27日，赴"音配像"现场途中逝世。 6月16日，中共中央领导乔石、李瑞环及首都各界人士向张君秋遗体告别。

Lifetime Events of Zhang Jun-qiu

1920	October 14th, 1920(September Third in lunar calendar): born in Beijing. Father, Teng Lian-fang, a clerk; Mother, Zhang Xiu-qin, a Chin Yi performer of Hebei Bangzi. Original name: Teng Jia-hong. He used his mother's surname since he became a performer.
1926~1932	Studying in the private school and school for ordinary people; performing in Baoding, Zhang Jiakou with his mother.
1933	Acknowledging Li Ling-feng as master to learn Chin Yi and studying *Color Building Match, Miss Su San Goes to Trail, Entering the Palace for the Second Time, Sacrificing at the Riverside*; his master's master Wang Yao-qing started to teach him.
1936	He made his first debut in "Fortune" theatre by performing *Miss Su San Goes to Trail*; performing in other people's troupe; performing *Great Palace* with Li Duo-kui; performing *Fa Men Temple* with Tan Xiao-pei, Hao Shou-chen, Ci Rui-quan; performing *Joint Hearing* with Jiang Miao-xiang; becoming student of Shang Xiao-yun; learning *The Match of Spring and Autumn, The Imperial Stele Pavilion*; performing *Qiankun Fushou Mirror, Jiu Qu Yellow River Lantern, Herd Boy and Spinning Girl* with Shang Xiao-yun in Chang Qing Troupe.
1937	From February to April, performing *Da Bao Guo, A Visit to the Tomb of Emperor, Entering the Palace for the Second Time, Si Lang Visits His Mother* in Chinese Theatre of Tianjin in Wang You-chen's troupe; performing *Si Lang Visits His Mother, The Imperial Stele Pavilion* with Meng Xiao-dong in Tianjin. May, performing *Prosperity Brought by the Dragon and the Phoenix, Fa*

Men Temple, Su Wu as a Shepherd, Four Scholars, Breeze Pavilion, The Fisherman's Revenge, Identifying the Head and Stabbing Tang with Ma Lian-liang in Golden Theatre in Shanghai in Fu Feng Troupe; acknowledging Mei Lan-fang as master in Shanghai and starting to learn *The Phoenix Returns to Its Nest, Farewell between Life and Death, Farewell My Concubine, Top of the Universe, Selling Horse*.

1938	February, performing in Tianjin in Wang You-chen's troupe.
	February, performing in Xin-xin Theatre in Beiping in Ma Lian-liang's troupe.
	March, performing in Chinese Theatre of Tianjin in Tan Fu-ying's Fu Chun Troupe.
	April, performing in Beiping Hua Le Theatre in Tan Fu-ying's Fu Chun Troupe.
	May, performing in Golden Theatre in Shanghai in Tan Fu-ying's Fu Chun Troupe.
	From June to July, learning Dan role from Feng Zi-he and Kunqu from Zheng Chuan-Jian and Zhu Chuan-ming while he was on holiday in Shanghai.
	August: performing in Shanghai in Ma Lian-liang's Fu Feng Troupe.
1938~1941	Performing most of the time in Ma Lian-liang's Fu Feng Troupe, also cooperating with Jin Shao-shan and Tan Fu-Ying; continuing his learning in Wang Yao-qing's home.
	Li Yan Illustrated widely seeking advice from readers and inviting social celebrities to agree on " Li Shi-fang, Mao Shi-lai, Zhang Jun-qiu and Song De-zhu as the Four Junior Great Female Role Players ".
1940	Marrying Zhao Yu-rong.
1941	Leaving Fu Feng Troupe, Fulfilling learning from Li Ling-feng.
	Cheng Yan-qiu teaching Zhang Jun-qiu plays such as *Legend of Zhu Hen, Legend of Hong Fu, Picture of Two Emperors*, and *Legend of a Golden Lock*.
1942	Establishing Qian He Troupe and acting as the chief role with his father-in-law Zhao Yan-kui as chairman; He Shun-xin joined Qian He Troupe, in the early time, Li De-shan played the erhu, He Shun-xin played the jinghu. Later, it was He Shun-xin who played the jinghu.
	Members of Qian He Troupe: Guan Sheng-xi, Zhang Chun-Yan, and Ji Yu-

liang played laosheng roles; Hou Xi-rui, Liu Lian-rong, Yuan Shi-hai and Wang Quan-kui played the painted-face roles; Jiang Miao-xiang, Ye Sheng-lan, Shang Fu-xia as Xiaosheng, Sun Yu-kun, Zhou Rui-an as Wusheng; Yan Shi-shan, Li Jin-hong played Peking Opera Blues; Li Duo-kui played Laodan; Xiao Chang-hua, Gao Fu-yuan and Xiao Sheng-xuan played Chou.

Representative plays: *Si Lang Visits His Mother, High-Spirited Horses with Red Long Hair, Fa Men Temple, The Imperial Stele Pavilion, Spring of Jade Hall, Sun Shang Xiang, Hatred of Li Zhu, Trap the Dragon Bed, Jin Shan Buddhist Temple, Broken Bridge and Lei Feng Pagoda, Da Bao Guo, Entering the Palace for the Second Time, Pass of Wu Zhao, Pass of Yan Gate, Pipa Reason, Hun Yuan Box, Ti Ying Saves Her Father, Farewell between Life and Death, The Phoenix Returns to Its Nest, Farewell My Concubine, Top of the Universe, Selling Horse, Wang Zhaojun's Marriage, Legend of Hong Fu, Legend of Zhu Hen, Legend of a Golden Lock.*

1943 His father Teng Lian-fang passed away.

September, Qian He Troupe performed *Spring of Jade Hall, Jin Shan Buddhist Temple, Broken Bridge and Lei Feng Pagoda, Wang Chun E, Si Lang Visits His Mother* in Tianjin.

November, Qian He Troupe performed *Spring of Jade Hall, Jin Shan Buddhist Temple, Broken Bridge and Lei Feng Pagoda, Wang Chun E, Si Lang Visits His Mother* in Shanghai. Teaching Gu Zheng-qiu *Wang Zhaojun's Marriage*.

1944 Marrying Wu Li-zhen.

September, disbanding Qian He Troupe.

1945~1947 Establishing Fall Troupe, acting as chairman and chief performer; innovating and acting *A Gentle Companion, Princess Yin Ping, Legend of Warriors*.

1948 Performing with Ma Lian-liang and Yu Zhen-fei in Pu Qing Theatre at Sun Lan-ting's invitation.

1949 Making opera-style film *Mei Long Town, The Fisherman's Revenge* with Ma Lian-liang and making opera-style film *Spring of Jade Hall* with Yu Zhen-fei at the invitation of Hong Kong victory film company.

Performing with Ma Lian-liang, Yu Zhen-fei, Cheng Zheng-tai, Wang Zheng-hua while staying in Hong Kong.

1951 October, returning to the mainland from Hong Kong.

1951~1952 Joining the Get-Together Central South Peking Opera Troupe in Wuhan;

	performing with Ma Lian-liang. Gao Sheng-lin, Gao Wei-lian, Guo Yuan-fen, Ye Sheng-mao and Zhang Jin-liang.
1952	Performing in Nanchang with Get-Together Central South Peking Opera Troupe via Tianjin to Beijing where he was received by Premier Zhou En-lai who encouraged him: " It is never too late to be patriotic, so is revolution. I hope you can make more contributions to our country." Establishing Beijing Get-Together Peking Opera, which was, renamed the Third Branch of Beijing Peking Opera Troupe. Members included: Chen Shao-lin, Gao Wei-lian, Ji Yun-lan, Li Si-guang, Zhu Jin-qin, Geng Shi-hua, Hao Qing-hai and Niu Rong-liang.
1953~1955	Innovating and acting *Liu Lan Zhi, The Legend of the Color Building*. Gao Wei-lian left the troupe and Liu Xue-tao joined in.
1956	Joining the delegation to give solicitude and salute to the Chinese People's Voluntary Army in Democratic People's Republic of Korea. *Riverside Pavilion* making its first appearance in Shanghai. Third Branch of Beijing Peking Opera Troupe merged with Ma Lian-liang Peking Opera Troupe and Second Branch of Beijing Peking Opera Troupe to set up Beijing Peking Opera Troupe. Members of Beijing Peking Opera Troupe: Chief performers: Ma Lian-liang, Tan Fu-ying, Zhang Jun-qiu and Qiu Sheng-rong. Laosheng: Chen Shao-lin, Ma Sheng-long, Liu Sheng-tong, Tan Yuan-shou, Ma Chang-li, Gao Bao-xian. Dan: Li Yu-fang, Li Shi-ji, Junior Wang Yu-rong. Xiaosheng: Liu Xue-tao, Ru Fu-hua, Min Zhao-hua. Jing: Zhou He-tong, Zhang Hong-xiang, Ma Chong-ren, Hao Qing-hai. Wusheng: Yang Sheng-chun, Huang Yuan-qing, Yang Shao-chun. Dansheng: Li Duo-kui, Geng Shi-hua. Chou: Ma Fu-lu, Ci Shao-quan, Li Si-guang, Guo Yuan-xiang, Niu Rong-liang.
1958	Innovating and acting *Concubine Zhen*. Making opera-style film *Riverside Pavilion*.
1959	Innovating and acting *Qiu Jin*. Innovating and acting *Qin Xiang Lian* (cooperating with Ma Lian-liang, Tan Fu-ying, Qiu Sheng-rong). Innovating and acting *The Orphan of the Zhao Family* (cooperating with Ma Lian-liang, Tan Fu-ying, Qiu Sheng-rong).

	Innovating and acting *The West Chamber* (cooperating with Ye Sheng-lan and Du Jin-fang from National Peking Opera Theatre of China).
1960	Innovating and acting *Made Made by scholar Number One* (cooperating with Ma Lian-liang, Tan Fu-ying).
1961	Innovating and acting *The Story in the Palace of Chu* (cooperating with Tan Fu-ying).
1962	Leading the performing group to perform with Wuhan Peking Opera Troupe)
	Innovating and acting *A Meeting of Poets*.
1963	Together with Ma Lian-liang and Qiu Sheng-rong, leading Beijing Peking Opera Troupe to perform *The Orphan of the Zhao Family, Qin Xiang Lian, Riverside Pavilion, Match Made by Scholar Number One, Selling Horse* in Hong Kong and Macao. Before leaving for Hong Kong, they performed *Riverside Pavilion* for Premier Zhou En-lai who later gave confirmation and modifying proposals to the performance. In mid-1965, producing opera-style film *Qin Xiang Lian*.
1964	Joining the group of directors of *Sparks of Reed Marshes*.
	Designing arias for the new play *Valley of Cherry-Apple* for the Experimental Peking Opera Troupe of Beijing.
1965	Transferring to the Second Branch of Beijing Peking Opera Troupe; innovating and acting *Prosperity* (cooperating with Ma Lian-liang).
1966~1967	Performances had to be stopped owing to the outbreak of the Cultural Revolution.
1968	His mother Zhang Xiu-qin passed away.
1969	His wife Wu Li-zhen passed away.
1970~1973	Resuming his job and joining the revising work of *The Red Detachment of Women, Battle on the Plain, The Legend of Red Lantern*.
1974	His wife Zhao Yu-rong passed away.
	Marring Xie Hong-wen.
1978	Transferring back to Beijing Peking Opera Troupe and resuming his stage life Summer of 1978: at Shi Ruo-xu's invitation, leading the Experimental Peking Opera of China Traditional Opera Institute to perform in Yantai; regaining the performance of *Miss Su San Goes to Trail*.
	Autumn of 1978: Conforming to the suggestions offered by Premier Zhou En-

Postscript

In memorial of the 85th birthday of Mr. Zhang Jun-qiu, this pictorial is published, according to the requirement of Mr. Li Rui-huan, by the editing committee of Zhang Jun-qiu, Master of Peking Opera, co-founded by Tianjin Chinese National Culture Promotion Association and Tianjin Zhang Jun-qiu Art Fund.

With Xie Hong-wen, Zhang Jun-qiu's wife, providing more than 600 pictures, this pictorial can be published. After repeated selection and consideration, we made it our editing idea that the pictorial should be in main progress with highlighting Zhang's glorious artistic achievements, his establishment of Zhang School, his training of Paking Opera performers, and his great contribution to the whole-hearted organization of audio-videotaping, with his development in art, his characteristics and dispositions running it through in both forms of words and pictures. In order to give an all-sided depiction of his whole brilliant life, great efforts have been made for a massive collection of his pictures and information. More than 900 pictures have been collected from where Zhang worked—The Central Academy of Drama and Beijing Peking Opera Theatres, and from Liu Xue-tao, He Shun-xin, Huang Zong-jiang, Lu Ji-ying, Shan Yao-zhu, Liu Zhang-jiang, Dai Tian-ping and Bai Jing-huan. In order to supply a want of Zhang's pictures in his adolescent life caused by events like Cultural Revolution, personnel has been organized to have found nearly 900 pictures, among which several dozens were selected, from *Li Yan Illustrated*, *The Bei-Yang Pictorial News*, *Ta Kung Pao*, *Shanghai News*, *Drama's World*, and *Pictorial of Latest News*. This task was strongly backed by Tianjin Library and Library of Nankai University, especially Lu Xing-su, the curator of Tianjin Library. In order to consummate this pictorial, a few valuable information from *People's Daily*, *Chinese Peking Opera* and *Popular Theatre* was collected. The current pattern has been formed on the basis of our repeated selection and consideration of the collected 2000 more pictures which may reflect our editing ideas.

Most of the pictures in the pictorial have never been published. The list of the plays, the characters, the background information and the years of the pictures were confirmed by Zhang's family members and relevant experts. Some were marked with exact years, while others, due to the unknown information, were marked with "such-and-such year". It was also true with the names of some characters. Experts are expected to do the correction.

Wang Wen-zhang, dean of Academy of Chinese Traditional Opera, Zhao Jing-bo, associate dean of The Central Academy of Drama and Wang Yu-zhen, dean of Beijing Peking Opera Theatres have contributed a lot to the information collection of the pictorial and to its editing and proofreading. Peking Opera Master Mr Liu Xue-tao not only provided a lot of very precious pictures but also made a careful investigation of the related historical events, which contributers greatly to the accomplishment and publishment of the picture album. Cai Ying-lian, professor of The Central Academy of Drama has provided many pictures for the pictorial, some of which were shot by herself.

At the publishing of this pictorial, we would like to express our sincere thanks to all the units and individuals who have provided pictures and consultation.

Our thanks also go to Lady Xie Hong-wen who, being ill, attached herself to planning and proofreading; to the children of Zhang Jun-qiu, especially Zhang Xue-jin, the nation-wide famous performing artist and Zhang Xue-hao, who has done a lot to carry forward the arts of Zhang Jun-qiu. Both of them have provided pictures and helped to proofread.

Leader of Tianjin Yangliuqing Fine Arts Press Mr. Liu Jian-chao and his teammates, after days of arduous work, successfully fulfilled the task by overcoming the difficulties of time limitation and heavy work in revision.

Due to our limited proficiency, information and time, careless omission is unavoidable and your forgiveness is kindly asked.

July 18, 2005

图书在版编目（CIP）数据

京剧大师张君秋 /《京剧大师张君秋》编委会编，
天津：天津杨柳青画社，2005.8
ISBN 7-80503-996-8
Ⅰ.京… Ⅱ.京… Ⅲ….张君秋（1920～1997）-
生平事迹-画册 Ⅳ.K825.78-64

中国版本图书馆 CIP 数据核字 (2005) 第 088560 号

京剧大师张君秋

出 版 人	刘建超
出 版 者	天津杨柳青画社
地　　址	天津市河西区佟楼三合里 111 号
邮政编码	300074
市场营销部电话	(022) 23346078　28374517　23352512
传　　真	(022) 23330487
邮购部电话	(022) 28350624
制　　版	杭州美虹电脑设计有限公司
印　　刷	深圳华新彩印制版有限公司
开　　本	787×1092 毫米　1/8
印　　张	44
版　　次	2005 年 10 月第 1 版
印　　次	2005 年 10 月第 1 次印刷
印　　数	1-2 000 册
字　　数	30 千字
书　　号	ISBN 7-80503-996-8/J.996
定　　价	880 元